The Student Handjob

So radical it's fucking bodacious

The Student Handjob.

Do you despise your gods? Have you filled your mouth with gin and butter, howled like a mangy fool at the disappearing prospect of the future? Good, good times, best times these. Filled the right forms, pressed the right buttons, wearing the correct underpants? Cleaned your teeth, said the right prayers, sanitised your Facebook page, adopted a fashionable hairstyle like all the other good girls and boys?

Over the next however many years we assume that you'll organise riots, explode information bombs, blackmail university managers, take real cool drugs, cheat the benefit system, barely work, steal prolifically, love manically, and learn to see a sorrowful new dawn with the grand, burnt retinas of highly deranged professors. The university, like the job market, like the economy, like too many things now is just a myth that most people consent to out of a combination of charming naivety and a grotesque lack of imagination. Learn to walk and talk with a nose-peg. We don't claim to know anything whatsoever but this guide might teach you a few new tricks.

University is all about turning tricks, anyway. Isn't it? Is it? Should it be? Partly? Is the knowledge brothel really safer than the street corner? Anyway, we don't hate the university. In fact, we are some of its biggest fans, which is why we want it to stop being a dick. Or a pissing contest. Or a madame, a pimp. A prophylactic against wage slavery maybe. Anyway, anyway, welcome, welcome, friends, foes, strangers and even strangerers, to the radical – so radical it's fucking bodacious – student handbook for students, etc....

[The Dancing] Table of [Dis]Contents:

Racism.

The university is a racist institution.

Face it. It's obvious. The answers are right in front of us. It is just that for a long time now nobody has bothered to ask the question. Racism does not function in every university in precisely the same way. It is played out differently according to the forces that shape each institution. Yet the overall impact is the same. Certain types of knowledge, like certain types of people, are deemed improper, unruly, and an imposition upon the smooth efficiency of the modern educational environment. These people, who tend to be 'of colour', are not let into some institutions en mass. Instead they are housed in academic ghettos. Here they are offered the chance to escape, to get out the ghetto. But only if they submit to training themselves to no longer be the problem. It's the price of the ticket.

This is why in, say, a Russell group university (let's name names, Oxford, UCL or Southampton) there are barely any non-white students. This is an outcome of having barely any non-white academics. In these institutions, courses on slavery, colonialism, black radical thought and black feminism, are thought to be an addendum to the teaching of the proper ideas of modernity. Those 'race' courses are specialisms to be taught by the one or two non-white academics the university has deemed capable of crossing the colour line. But that is all they are limited to. These academics are the 'race' people, intended to keep the few 'race' students happy. The only significant numbers of non-whites seen in Russell Group institutions are those who clean the toilets and work the security desk. They cross into the colonial fort when others leave and keep the thing running.

Go to the other end of the scale. To those ghettos towards the bottom of the University League table (London Met, University of East London, Thames Valley University). The majority of students here are non-white. Funnily enough these institutions are also amongst the most poorly funded. But this does not mean all the thought that is excluded from the Russell Group finds a home here. Instead this type of university covers its gaping cracks by placing posters of people who resemble their student body over the walls. These posters yell declarations at the student, telling her that there is much to be gained from this institution if only she grasps the opportunity. This university ghetto is her chance to get out of the other ghetto. She can become an accountant, a physiotherapist or even set up her own business. All this can be achieved without studying the massive dislocations of the slave trade and settler colonialism. Who needs to learn about that shit, anyway? It's over and done with, isn't it?

Do not believe what the university has to say about equal opportunities and diversity. Ignore the rainbow nation chromatism of its homepage. This is just a bullshit cover for the university's real crimes of exclusion. Racism is not over because it is covered by legislation. So the next time an academic publishes an article about how black women are the ugliest creatures around, and the most the university is prepared to do is publicly wag it's finger at him and tell him not to do it again, be prepared. Be prepared and get together. Be prepared to get together and talk about what needs to be done.

Perhaps even be prepared to cause some trouble. Holler. Scream. Make a list of demands. You've got nothing to lose. Whichever university you are in, it only ever sees you as a problem. So go ahead an act like one.

Shitting the desk: how to hack a classroom.

Think of the structure of an ordinary class: students pay to learn, teachers are paid to teach. A customer seeks value for money: the commodity, 'knowledge'. What is learned and exchanged is expertise, the content of the class: Biochemistry, Critical Theory, English Romantic Literature, etc. How is this content acquired? As something transmitted, 'knowledge' becomes independent of both teacher and student - an object. This 'knowledge' is solely possessed by the teacher, inaccessible to the student unless they can successfully emulate the gestures and ideas of the teacher. If knowledge is power then the student begins at a profound disadvantage. No matter how hard the student works this knowledge is always at a critical remove, and when the student thinks they understand the subject, further training is needed - an MA, MRes, PhD, post-doc, and so on.

The classroom is a place where the student must passively smile and nod appropriately as the wise teacher defines knowledge. A sleep-inducing teacher is simply misunderstood - concentrate harder, 'umm' and 'hmm' louder, push that dictaphone even closer to their furrowed brow and napkin-scrawled lecture notes. The classroom fixes two adults, the teacher and student, into a very specific power relation. It is this inequality that brings the student, that seeker of knowledge, to the university in the first place. Its institutional structure gives marks and degrees their value and legitimacy, convincing later employers that this course of study has officially recognised merit.

Of course this does not mean that an entirely cynical approach should be taken towards study. Teachers may be genuinely interested in discussing ideas, just don't be fooled by the rhetoric of 'learning together', of 'inspirational experience', of 'achieving insights'. These things might all happen, but they are not inherent to the structure described above. Even where alternative forms of learning and assessment are promised, even where assessment itself is being questioned in its objectivity, most of the time these 'alternatives' simply cover up a real structure of inequality. This structure has concrete purposes. In several important regards, university and its knowledge have the function of reinforcing gaps - between people, classes, genders -- and reinforcing and dressing up power structures. This, and not the content that is taught, becomes the truth of university. *Mind the gap....*

Disempowered by the classroom, to the point of being a passive hearing node to the lecturer's drawl, the student might attempt some petulant

revenge. "Only 69%? Where is my value for money? I pay your salary sir, madam. I'll tell the marketing director/mummy that you failed to use Powerpoint or update the virtual learning zone." The customer service model has been rolled out in education, healthcare and social services in order to begin their privatisation into profit-making businesses. On the one hand, the arrogance of the classroom and its power relations; on the other, the naïve resentment and dangerous arrogance of seeing university as a product a customer pays for, where ideas become equivalent to purchasing a hoover or gastric bypass. Either one involves shitting the desk. Better to do away with desks altogether.

Consider that old saying, 'she who cheats only cheats herself?' Bollocks! The classroom is a game where the rules and pieces are all open to adjustment, though care must be taken to get away with it. Most of the time though, awareness of the structures makes cheating unnecessary anyway. Address the structure as it wants to be addressed (e.g. pretending that you are learning for yourself and not for others - another one of those infamous proverbs of pedagogy whose inversion reveals more than they can possible be happy with) and get your fix of knowledge elsewhere (the section on organisation can provide you helpful tools for that → organisation). Knowledge, in fact, is everywhere. Theory begins before the student even steps into the library for the first time. Theory comes from the Greek word *theoria* and means nothing other than seeing. An everyday activity, no? By understanding theory as a form of abstraction (biologically involved in the very act of seeing) then we can see how actually everything involves theoretical presuppositions, even if they are not explicit. Think how a map is read or a supermarket navigated, how three people make a meal or how flirtation operates. So if everything involves these kind of theoretical presuppositions why should some have the status of a specialized and carefully guarded knowledge depending on a class of experts and their teaching? - which brings us back to the monopolizing institution called university. Considered from this perspective the monopoly becomes quite contestable doesn't it? *Mind the gap, but never mind the bollocks!*

This power-knowledge dynamic is hard to side-step: whilst knowledge can be spread in more equal and effective means in reading and study groups, courses have to be completed and a certain collusion is necessary with the classroom. Learning is a relation and an activity between two or more individuals: not all teaching is learning, but neither is learning something that can be paid for. The university is more than a teaching/training machine. The classroom can be disillusioning, first year drop-out rates are high. You'll learn an equal amount, if not more, from other students than teachers. Self-critique, convictions, openness and independent thinking are more useful than most textbooks, but can leave a bad smell in a classroom. Use carefully. University is not for everyone but it is important to remember there is more to be gained than what is said in lectures. Mind the gap, tolerate the bollocks, and instead of shitting the desk, dispense with desks altogether. Learning is a relation, not a currency. The classroom is a state of mind.

Beat up or beat off?

♥♥ Your teacher and You ♥♥

As with all bourgeois institutions, the university is intimately concerned with calculating and ordering: hierarchy worked out to the Nth degree. You are a 64, she is a 65. That boy over there in the flawless knitwear, his parents are academics, he, my friend, is a 74. She has some good views about Kant, but completely fails to learn the lessons of Foucault, or something. He has published a book but it is widely thought to be mediocre. She is a tenured professor, she is only a junior lecturer. That wretched little creature over there, a second year student. Yuck, listen to its poorly formed opinions. Click, whir, everything must be put in order. Everything and everyone must know its place. It's OK, the conveyor belt takes us up the ranks. Keep your forehead still so it doesn't smudge when you are stamped with your grade. Alight here for an MA in being better than an undergrad student, but still a long way off the glorious misery of the PhD. Well, yes, people fall off into the machinery all the time. Don't worry, the university hires C+ psychologists to run around with safety nets, staunching the bloodflow from the course completion rate. Anyway, as long as you have money you'll be fine. Do you have money? Can I borrow some?

This university is better ranked than that one. Its research output is of a first world-class standard. That one is basically a polytechnic in disguise. Pfft. That one up there, you can just make out its turrets through the mist, it is one of the best in the world. It has accepted six or seven black students in the last ten years. Each of its colleges has a gift shop. Just think. If we work hard at a good university, one day, we will be able to work for a worse one. Imagine it, my friend - an office with our name on the door. Still, people will snigger when they see our rank and institution sutured to our name on conference programmes, our place within the machine inscribed indelibly upon our bodies of work.

Still, in our wildest, most fervid, wettest dreams we might eventually become professors, those very good people, those people who are innately better than us. Have you quoted their latest monograph in your essay, offering the lightest of light criticism? Well done, good boy, good girl. Professors have read a great deal and have very good opinions. Because of this, it is very hard for them to listen to you. They moved beyond your opinions a long time ago. You are naïve, ill informed, in poor taste. They want to listen, but you are boring, mildly irritating at best. Although your flesh is young and firm, interesting, to them. 'How very fucking interesting! You must come to one of my dinner parties. Here, have some more wine.'

Most students will have very few contact hours with a professor – and a 20-minute session snatched can lead to frustration, brown-nosing, or, towards new ideas, inspirations and directions. A professor can, often without realising it, make or break one's academic experience. Professors are all different, of course, but without exception they have magnificent egos: large, proud, fragile. They will not be seen to agree or learn from you, and flagrant disagreements over some academic heresy will result in headaches and unfairly reduced marks. Frustration and demoralisation can be avoided in the university hierarchy by not seeking approval from a professor for the sake of it. By remaining independent, a student can pursue her own lines of research within the academy provided she knows the tacit rules of academic pissing/funding contests, and how to avoid being cornered into massaging a professor's ever-wounded pride (or anything else for that matter).

Strong relationships with professors are effective, reassuring and lucrative – and a thorough ego-massage plays a key part in obtaining references. Yet, the average professor is a grown-up student with deep-seated anxieties of being publicly exposed as a bluffing fraud. Sensitive egos, hard shells, bilious venom. A student seeking top marks can easily manipulate their essay so that it conforms to course content and the research interests of the lecturer. Professors are in competition with each other to produce quality work and like it when students engage with it. But this kind of mediocre research sets up students for a life of masturbating over other peoples' ideas, inevitably resulting in the tiresome identity crises visible in many academics. Whilst not beating off your teacher, beating up a teacher isn't so sensible either. Once the mystique of a teacher's divine wisdom is shattered, the student is in a position to assert himself as an up and coming pointy head. But quoting too much of an obscure author, talking over the teacher or excessively patronising other students can result in disfavour.

Students are more numerous, this is their strength. Gang up, conspire, work together, don't kick each other down. Engage, teach, learn amongst each other, challenge seminar egos. Make hierarchy subordinate to friendship. Um, what? ... Oh yeah, never mind. Tell them to fuck off with their cranial measurements and towing of the baited hook, line and sinker. Be aware of how hierarchies work - they're not going anywhere, so work together, not against each other. Even professors look over their shoulders at the PR-hogs and management dunces now cutting their budgets in half in some latest productivity drive. At least be alert to it. Play the game, stroke their egos, but never without the knowing that they require you to believe in their status for them to feel the warmth of superiority. You don't live in a glasshouse, but a handful of stones can easily be gathered together. Safety in numbers. There may be a determined mastery of the student by the teacher, but this, wherever possible, should be broken. Only in this way does learning become possible within the university.

We are not interested in moderation.

Crime...

Sometimes I wonder what strange fate brought me out of the storm to that house that stood alone in the shadows. As I probed into its mysteries every clue told me a different story, but each had the same ending - university. Suddenly a flashback punctures the narrative.

"Being a paragon of virtue can only last so long kid. A riot, a meltdown, spinning drunken yarns of your tough childhood. It doesn't matter now. There're too many martyrs already. Schmucks who'd rather suffer and save face. The future's been stolen, only a fool or a martyr would cling to the old rules now."

You see we're criminalised from the outset. Watched, monitored, accounted for. Indebted. We have no money for the present or the future, no time either. This ain't a hipster endorsement of hey yah cool crime. You've already been criminalised whenever you step out of beat - overstaying your visa, signing on whilst working cash-in-hand to save up, claiming housing benefit while studying more than sixteen hours a week, posting bad jokes on Facebook, not touching out, not touching in, using a Blackberry... We are not criminals but neither are we good dancers.

Cop shows are full of clichés; detectives are maverick loners, jazz playing, sports-car driving alcoholics with a tough exterior but a rock solid conscience. He'll be smooth yet OCD (and as a pro-crime fighter he'll surely be a he - although women apparently make good amateurs, or else occasionally obstinate rule-sticklers who need to be bypassed...), either that or he'll have some other 2D gimmick instead of a personality, but hey, he's a great cook and the broads love him - especially those impossibly wasp-waisted ones in constant peril, spooked by stalkers and snatched by mobsters.

Good cop bad cop is only half right. In reality they are pretty much all psycho, they joined the cops for starters. There have been about 1500 deaths in UK police custody, pursuits or shootings since 1990. Did these people die of old age? Had an allergic reaction to a peanut they were offered during interrogation? To put that in perspective, that's roughly double the amount of British Soldiers killed in conflict during the same period (that's Iraq I & II, Afghanistan, Northern Ireland, Sierra Leone and the Balkans put together).

... or How to Write a Shit Detective Story – (a serial)

There are however a few plots typical of the policed Academy that we have serialised for you here – these will make a far more interesting storyline for that creative writing assignment you've been set. So, for inspiration, these are a few screenplays we dug up from the university library, filed under the section 'crime fiction'. You know the ones - the embittered student, pissed off at the world, decides to imagine themselves as the anti-hero of their own pulp crime novel.

Episode 1: Cadfael goes Kojaking Inspector Morse's Shaft

The anti-hero, Steve Cadfael (BA Latin and Theology joint hons), attempts to sell some gear to his wet-eared, slap-headed monk buddies down at that most traditional of universities, the monastery. Princesses, geeks, abbots, they all have their poison, so brother Cad sets about finding out what his flatmates are into (khat and plant fertilisers are somewhat passé, he discovers). He starts off scoring some himself from local dealers, getting a sense of who has what and a few numbers. From there he increases the bulk slowly - he has a loan after all – selling to friends and friends of friends who happily pay for the convenience. In no time at all he has paid off all of his student debt to the Sheriff of Nottingham and consequently has plenty of time available for all sorts of ungodly activities involving brother Morse's shaft.

Drugs.

Liberal Democracy

Pushed by extremely well funded gangs and cartels, this one is a properly nasty little fucker, responsible for a great deal of violence internationally and within nations. Causes the delusion of something known as 'individual freedom', and also the belief that voting every few years for one of two groupings of the same bunch of rich kids, distinguished only by arbitrary colours, amounts to taking part in politics.

High - Causes feelings of immense superiority over other people, and is marked by a rabid hypocrisy, or flickering schizophrenia, between the ideals it espouses and their complete negation in actual behaviour. If institutional racism and sexism, schizophrenia, and psychotic episodes of imperialism are your sort of buzz, then this one is for you.

Communism

Extremely hard to get a hold of these days. May in fact be the stuff of urban legend. Fake syntheses proliferate - look for people selling newspapers - but generally fall short of expectations, causing only paranoia and authoritarian impulses.

High - Allegedly brings about the removal of exploitation, the loss of alienation, and feelings of community and communion with others. I have only experienced tip-of-the-tongue tastes of it in the flashes of fleeting moments of collective action, to date. Suggests deep sustenance and the liberation of human potential.

Anarchism

Much talk of this in recent times. Has been used to refer to any number of substances and things of little substance. For some people it apparently causes the irrational fear of people in black (not to be confused with the fear of black people: see Liberal Democracy, above) unravelling the social fabric. In others it brings about the determined belief that The State is inherently bad, and extremely bad for the health (of society).

High - A sugary rush of political agency. Yet to be seen if that high can be sustained. If you're at a demo, cover your face and follow the red and black flag for a smashing night/day on the town. If not, probably best to try and score it off someone who doesn't look like the MTV version of an anarchist. Harder to recognise, but worth the effort for a better buzz.

Capitalism

Like a big fat bag of crack, free of charge when you're young, bored and impressionable. It's legal too, despite causing more damage than everything else combined, so no need to worry about the cops: they're hooked on the glass cock too. The sickly sweet siren call of this one doesn't so much make you smash against the rocks, but makes you pimp-out and prostitute yourself so you can buy more rocks of it. Job in a call centre, anyone? Unless you're born into money, in which case you get to fuck the life out of everyone else. Wouldn't want to be you when they decide they've had enough, though.

High – A shallow, yet impossible to satiate desire for more and more shit at the cost of everything else. A bit like Prozac, it covers over a complex and undulating unhappiness with a shallow, artificial evenness. A kind of hypnosis that disguises the crushing boredom of the continual repetition of the same with flashing, candy coloured lights and auto-tuned emotions.

Utopianism

This one is designed to blow the backdoor, front door, hell, even the walls, off your imagination. Bang one under your tongue, free your mind and head off out to lunch. Food will taste better, sex will be more pleasurable, and the sea will taste of lemonade. You might appear to others as if you're a few sandwiches short of a picnic, though. Imagining better worlds can be a powerful pastime. Just remember that imagining something doesn't mean it exists. Use your excursions into the beautiful unknown to criticise the miserable state of the world as it is, now. We all know what happens to people who try to hide away in Neverland with a chimp for a best friend: nothing very fucking good.

High – 'There will be 37 million poets the equal of Walt Whitman, 37 million musicians the equal of Nina Simone, and 37 million mathematicians the equal of Albert Einstein. Sex will be terrific, especially for transgendered people, with all tastes catered for. Food will be three times more delicate, delicious and plentiful than now. Cheese will flow in the rivers and we will...' Easy mate! You just stood in a massive runny dogshit and I'm worried you're going to check if it tastes like chocolate.

Socialism

An entry level treatment for most is this one. In many cases it is a gateway substance to more exploratory ideals. Others can have a bad trip and never come back to this kind of medication. It has proved a keeper though - campuses across the island are flooded with the sweet smell of this toxin. Be warned: they'll try to get you on this young and will react if you fancy another tipple. Once you find your supplier you'll easily find them again, or more likely they'll find you. Variants of the same strand are everywhere but regulars usually maintain a cult like devotion to one. You can spot an addict by their dissident superiority complex and endless begging for money.

High - Here is a classic case where you can never quite match the first buzz. Feelings of euphoria and arrival to some higher plain may be replaced by anxiety and nausea after sustained use. Users feel a tendency to sit in meetings and discuss what's going on outside, but fear looking out of the window. Can also induce authoritarian feelings of one-ness. Many spend their high trying to get everyone else hooked. Side effects also include a desire to write endless dribble in papers and an aggressive, nostalgic but irrelevant interest in history.

Situationism

Probably doesn't exist nowadays, if it ever did at all. The stuff of rumour and marketing, a brand name frequently applied to multiple sub-standard knock-offs, mostly placebos. Drug of choice for arty and media types, its effects are fleeting and rarely match the hype. Nevertheless it remains the stuff of legends, is frequently highly addictive, especially amongst the young, and is freely available over the internet. A bit like plant food really. Be warned though, prolonged users are likely to loose their inhibitions, possibly their self-respect, and will find it difficult to be taken seriously.

High - Often results in the unpleasant development of egotistical tendencies and attention seeking behaviour. Produces intense emotions ranging from euphoria to disorientation and confusion. Frequent users have been reportedly found aimlessly wandering the streets for days, even months on end. Causes alterations in spatial perception, breathlessness of prose and linguistic deformations.

Time and space.

People tell you to manage your time. Perhaps time is not to be managed – perhaps it is to be liberated. To be made into really free time. This happens when we appreciate how time is open and how it is closed, which time we can control and which is ordered by powers that for now, we cannot. University gives us a unique opportunity to experiment with time. In the workaday world we seem to only be able to tinker at the edges, faking sickness, dodging fares, modulating our boredom threshold. Essentially, unless we can stake out a means of surviving other than work: squatting, 'skipping' for food, stealing, or rich patrons perhaps, then time manages us rather than the other way around. On the face of it such options to reclaim time can seem pretty hardcore, and not everyone wants to go down those routes. Still, we can do worse than remember that work turns our time into a commodity to be bought and sold, apportioned and packaged, invested and wasted, from holidays and leisure to labour per hour or per annum. *Arbeit does not macht frei*, it keeps us chained, and it is such chains we stand to lose by freeing our time.

For the capitalists calling the shots, university is an investment in the future, time spent studying will pay off later. To liberate university time requires a rethink: you've bought yourself some time out of the control of full-time employment, so now to waste it in new and glorious ways, not in consumable packets - TV shows and taxi rides - but to open it to exploration and the unpredictable. If you don't waste money on stupid shit you have to work less and can live your time rather than kill it. Lived time is exploring, it's understanding, it's cooking and eating, it's walking, it's friendships, relationships, it's drifting aimlessly, it's going to the park and sometimes it's remembering that history hasn't ended.

This is what is propitious about university time. It can often be free and freely wasted, it can be explored and opened, rearranged and redirected to all manner of unproductive activities. It gives us that time to try to make some history for a change, or to support those doing so. This is one of the best things about university and the thing that the scum in power are trying to crush, enclose and marketise through the weapon of debt - a kind of mutually assured destruction. 'You waste our time and we'll waste yours, welcome to your bleak future, time is money after all'. So for now, we manage with what we've got, those scraps of time cast off from the banquet of fat cats and capitalist pigs, tossed our way so begrudgingly so as to just about keep us alive – they need us to sleep, to consume, and to be kept amused or else the whole circus is going up in flames.

So how to liberate time? The answer lies in something perhaps less obvious, but just as important in shaping the university experience – space. Space, its all around us, its pretty mind-blowing to think that at this exact moment a trillion simultaneous events are unfolding across it, it's changing every second. University space, like time, is also distinctive. Understanding this helps us liberate it.

Space too can be enclosed: rooms, campuses and whole cities are laid out in particular configurations to engineer behaviour; transport systems are nakedly classist, affording mobility to the rich and isolation to the poor. The university itself is enmeshed in an international spatial web of finance, research and reputation, halls of residence are often a tightly policed rip-off and private landlords are almost without exception a despicable class who will attempt all means possible to steal your money. But university space is open too. The space of the university is produced by you, the student – this gives you power if you are organised. For all the managers and lecturers, cleaners and caterers, the resources and buildings, the social and cultural relations, the charter and the capital, without the student the university is nothing. You can occupy, hold meetings, disrupt, but also inhabit differently, mindful of the fact that the space is produced by you: use it, appropriate, turn up to the corporate receptions, art show openings and graduations and get the free wine, divert the wealth of facilities to divergent ends - from the books and DVDs in the library (learn what you aren't meant to, copy and pass on), to the computers, the printing facilities, the sports fields, the workshops and the spaces themselves. The university can become your playground but so, too, can the city itself.

If you find yourself at university in a new city then you're lucky, the expense of moving away means it's not an option open to all. The disorientation and discovery can be intoxicating in many ways, but knowing your geography is likewise an indispensable tactic for getting by. So do reconnaissance, know your city, know your enemy and know your friends.

Exploring space is about finding safe places, and dangerous ones, finding escape routes, orientating yourself to local contexts. It's confidence, it's solidarity, it's seeing the structures at work that shape our lives and the power behind them. It can bring out thoughts, patterns, connections; the city is not a stage, it's a writhing snakepit: dive in and get to know it. Go off piste, get pissed, go for a walk, watch your back. Scout the security, notice the passageways, spot places to squat, find the shops where they chuck out bags of sandwiches at closing time, find the stations without gates, notice the bus routes where it's possible to get on without passing the driver. If you're planning street protests or direct action for any reason, knowledge of the space (and time of day you are aiming for) is one of your most potent weapons. Know your enemy: power has all sorts of ways of policing our time and space, so explore them, find ways around. Sometimes go in disguise - this might be a mask or a hoodie, at other times a business suit - both can get you out of a tight spot in various circumstances. Prepare, be aware of your footprints, and your electronic ones. Be paranoid but don't be intimidated. Use an unregistered sim, misspell your name, pay cash. Walk, if you can't then cycle, if you can't then get a bus; transport costs usually increase in inverse relation to the time a journey takes, but not only is the quicker transport more expensive, it's more disorientating, the best way to know a space is on foot. Having said that, different people experience space differently, if personal safety is a concern then hunt in packs. Know your friends, meet people, talk, encounter. A city can be a giant game, a never-ending discovery, but be aware of your social position. University students can be a vanguard of colonisation, the middle-class appropriation of working class spaces, opening them up, making them safe and trendy so that property developers can move in, landlords can hike the rent and kick the residents out to make way for organic cafés, 'pop-up' art galleries and expensive bars. Be aware of this, if you think you are gentrifying, stop. Space is alive and socially constructed, when we become aware of this our relation to it and its other inhabitants can change for the better. Perhaps the best way to make your time really free is to live without dead space.

University doesn't have to be about investing in future earnings, it can be a time and space away from the more ordered and controlling spacetime of family, school and work. The university is not apart from the world or society, somehow detached, but rather utterly enmeshed within it, its struggles and its power relations. However, even in the face of recent shitty assaults from the government, it can still be a time and space seized back from the more enclosed and marketised situations we encounter elsewhere in life, an experiment in living differently. Perhaps the best way to inhabit university is to make use of time and space, rather than to merely consider them as bargaining chips to be exchanged for property or other space-time configurations.

Don't consume space, produce it. Don't buy time, take it.

Crime, Episode 2: Quincy shows his Ironside to Poirot's Cracker

Biology student, Peter Quincy, attempts to blackmail his teacher and eminent French theorist, Prof. Poirot, at the Christmas party, and then again at a post-conference piss-up. As is a time-honoured lecturer tradition, the lecherous Prof. Poirot tries it on with the not-so-hapless Quincy. Against his better instinct Quince takes this where it goes, but doesn't get too pissed, making sure to reliably document the evidence, recording the passionate petting on his phone, and getting his mates to snatch a few incriminating snaps. Quincy then uses old Poirot's facebook account to track down his long-suffering spouse, as well as finding the details for the head of department and the Uni's head of HR. Clever Quince knows to ask for the cash up front, but assumes that grades are part of the deal too, naturally. Continually upping the stakes, pausing only to recite the plot of Lolita to cheer poor Poirot up, Quincy informs him 'it's not me, it's your 50K salary.' He is soon enjoying fruity cocktails in Marbella.

Depression.

Much is said of how to cope with depression. How to survive it, deal with it, manage it. How to see a light/carrot at the end of the tunnel. Nothing much is said of the tunnel itself.

Do things you enjoy, share your feelings with loved ones, take each day as it comes, listen to Tony Robbins while you sleep... What use is this advice when relationships with family, friends, teachers, are so thoroughly colonised by the forms of sociability and production which lead to these feelings in the first place? How do you deal with the fact that your family is investing in you and expect a return? Or that the state no longer sees you as worth the investment, except as a producer of perpetual debt? How can we cope with the subtle yet enforced competition against our friends for good marks? With being instructed by superiors in the proper way to critique power? How can you answer family friends who ask what you're going to *do* with your arts degree?

Despite talk of the post-industrial West, we are still on the production line – only the produce has changed. Instead of cars, toothpaste and toys we produce desire, debt, careers and websites. And for those of us who still insist on being bookish, we produce Academic Excellence. For what purpose? IT research for efficiency. Medical research for profit and longer (working) lives. Sociological research for coffee tables. And psychological research for managing human resources. Psychology, via its current favourite child Cognitive Behavioural Therapy, no longer has time to impose its own fruity theories on our minds, but rather has been employed to implement the most efficient, no-nonsense methods for getting us back-up-and-running, working, writing essays, socialising, carrying on. It tells us that negative feelings are solely a result of negative thoughts. This theory has seeped into the HR imagination, where workers are commanded to see forced redundancy "as an opportunity", with the pathological cheerfulness of a corporate team-building weekend.

I don't mean to write off CBT altogether – once a certain stage of paralysis has been reached, changing the way you think can enable you to imagine and to start to create different social and productive relations. And that's just the point. Why do we need well-meaning psych-grads with sympathetic eyebrows asking us about our childhoods in six sessions? (Only four during peak-times, such as exam-time – get in early!) What is needed is a type of optimism that will cut through the powerlessness of that's-the-way-it-is-deal-with-it oppression that will afford us an emancipatory creativity and a rabid imagination. The depression and alienation often felt when critiquing the systems which shape our lives is symptomatic of our Human Centipede- education, with those in front of us crapping in our mouths only for us to do the same to those behind us.

The idea that until some utopia magically appears we all have to be drugged up to the eyeballs and be told what we're feeling and why is deeply problematic. This model of being "guided" and "self" helped (which never actually comes from your self, but rather from some expert) is disheartening and only ever aims for personal, individual "happiness" - that is, coping with an exploitative working life. I'm not trying to find a cure or guide people through clinical depression - there are thousands of bestsellers doing that. I'm saying that people can think for themselves about the mechanisms of exploitation in which they find themselves and organise collectively around that. To find that you, yourself, can articulate your own experience without resorting to dictated psychology-management speak can be more empowering than repeating self-affirmation mantras cooked up by some self-appointed hack with an expensive smile.

Hacking.

On 15 February 2003 over 1 million people marched on a cool Saturday afternoon to show their opposition to the invasion of Iraq and voice their frustration with politicians who had ignored their concerns. Despite the march, the obvious government-media collusion, and, the clearly dodgy intelligence, the British campaign continued for six more years.

On 26 March 2011 over 1 million people marched on another Saturday afternoon to express their opposition to a grinding package of cuts, redundancies and the marketisation of education, voicing their frustration with politicians ... yeah, you get it. Again, nothing changed. The April 2011 budget cuts whistled through. Our cities, jobs and communities implode and burn.

The political march, the rally and the petition have been often established by recent events as a well-meaning waste of time and energy. Information, representation and data are by far the most important commodities today – no longer votes but share prices, market confidence, digitised flows of information between billions of nodes, most managed by a few huge information cartels – Google, Amazon, Apple, Facebook, Microsoft. Strikes work by damaging or depriving the powerful of an essential part of their capital accumulation – traditionally labour. But now that primary production of material commodities has also been augmented by the gathering and processing of information, an abstracted capital, so then disruption and damage to information networks has become an additional tactic of increasing relevance for political protest and subversion.

Hacking is what we're talking about. So, as well as showing solidarity with Palestinians by protesting outside the embassy with your buddies or making a racket outside some hapless shop on a Saturday afternoon, why not show your comrades some extra support – by bringing down a news server, by leaking information, causing chaos online? You don't have to abandon your old campaigns but you may well be able to serve them best in other ways. Shut down Israeli Defence Force telecommunications anyone?

A quick Google search will tell you where to start: LulzSec, Distributed Denial of Service attacks. Stay anonymous, these people will try to make you disappear if you fuck with them – use proxys, public computers, USB sticks. Avoid wireless networks where possible. Use multiple identities, multiple email accounts. And when you join the digital revolution, remove any personal information you have online anyway – Facebook, LinkedIn and Twitter are all ways to lose your identity. Anonymity is strength. Remember that hacking works in reverse too – more likely than not the authorities are already employing technology to digitally comb your Facebook for things like obviously light-hearted references to public disorder, your Twitter for mentions of innocent water pistol fun. And, of course, it's not only the tabloids who are able to hack phones - tracking your location coordinates, or reading your encrypted chat messages (iPhone vs Blackberry - choose your poison/security level...).

Remember when you search the internet, the internet also searches you and each search logs the location of your Internet address and leaves a trace. The way things are going, it is much more likely it will be you, rather than Andy Coulson, that ends up being 'rushed through courts' in order to ensure the public of their safety - information safety or maybe safety through (dis-)information.

Tool up today. Swap the black hoodie for a hard drive and your smart(?)phone for a battered basic Finnish handset from 2001 - it has the added (Free Bonus feature!) advantage of holding only a dozen messages at any one time. We don't have all the answers for this stuff so learn the detail before you act. But if there's one thing a teenager from the Shetland islands can teach us it's that Hacking is the new Black Bloc and the trolls will always be playing catch-up.

Crime, Episode 3: Miss Marple plucks her Pink Panther for the big Hawaii 5-O

Tired of a town that's more big sleep than big smoke and weary of playing with her pink panther, Marple, a literature student at Oxbridgeingham Mansion of the Humanities (Private University), decides fuck it, she's bored, she's going to burn down a few banks and supermarkets. Apparently they have lots of money and useful things in them so she whacks up a few flyposters around the local area advertising a local smash and grab event, calls the local radio and makes sure she gets the local troubled NEETs down. They'll distract the cops with their lumpen ways, she muses, getting cuffed whilst she uses the mask of bourgeois respectability to grab herself some excellent homewares and fine cheeses.

Directing the action.

The University library is full of books that deconstruct, demystify and critique power structures. Chances are you may consider taking this to a more practical level. You get a petition circulating, you set up a meeting group, you go on a Saturday afternoon protest, and probably, you see the police violence. In the next day's paper, overblown reports of violent thugs, anarchists and sick elements causing disorder.

Truth is always a weapon - and so, questioning the state's monopoly on violence can be both liberating and empowering, and a helpful tool in political struggle. We do not believe the propaganda, which describes a demonstrator's broken skull as part of the necessary task of 'restoring order', while some broken windows are the deeds of a 'violent, criminal, a-political minority'.

There is a violence beneath everyday life. We can see how violence is part and parcel of a power system and the foundation of class difference. In fact, the term 'violence' is an imprecise term, contaminated by its political use to protect the state's monopoly on 'just' and legal violence. It is important to question this on all levels and not to restrict our resistance to well-mannered demonstrations and petitions. But not every form of political violence or direct action used by non-state groups is always helpful, legitimate or adequate.

Firstly, the communicability of actions should be considered. This does not mean we should do things just when we are sure that the mass media will approve - far from it, they will likely label us 'mindless thugs' anyway. But nevertheless, it is important to at least try to carve out an intrinsically political context for struggle. It might not always be about communicability but it might be about strategy. This also means that motives like vengeance or the drive to punish somebody for being a 'nasty capitalist' can be problematic. Are we targeting a system or bad individuals? Perhaps an attack on a government building is preferable to an attack on some of its representatives? That is not for us to judge, history teaches us all sorts of lessons, ideology others and ethics others still. Only you know your ends and your means, just think about it carefully.

Is violence legitimate? There's a constant violence inscribed in daily life. In the surveillance and security architecture, in increasing poverty, in police murders, in the collusion of MPs and bankers to keep a destructive system going. Violence shrouds the attacks on social services, the media offensive against criminals and rioters, benefits-cheats, or just benefit claimants, 'callous' immigrants daring to try to improve their lives and feed their

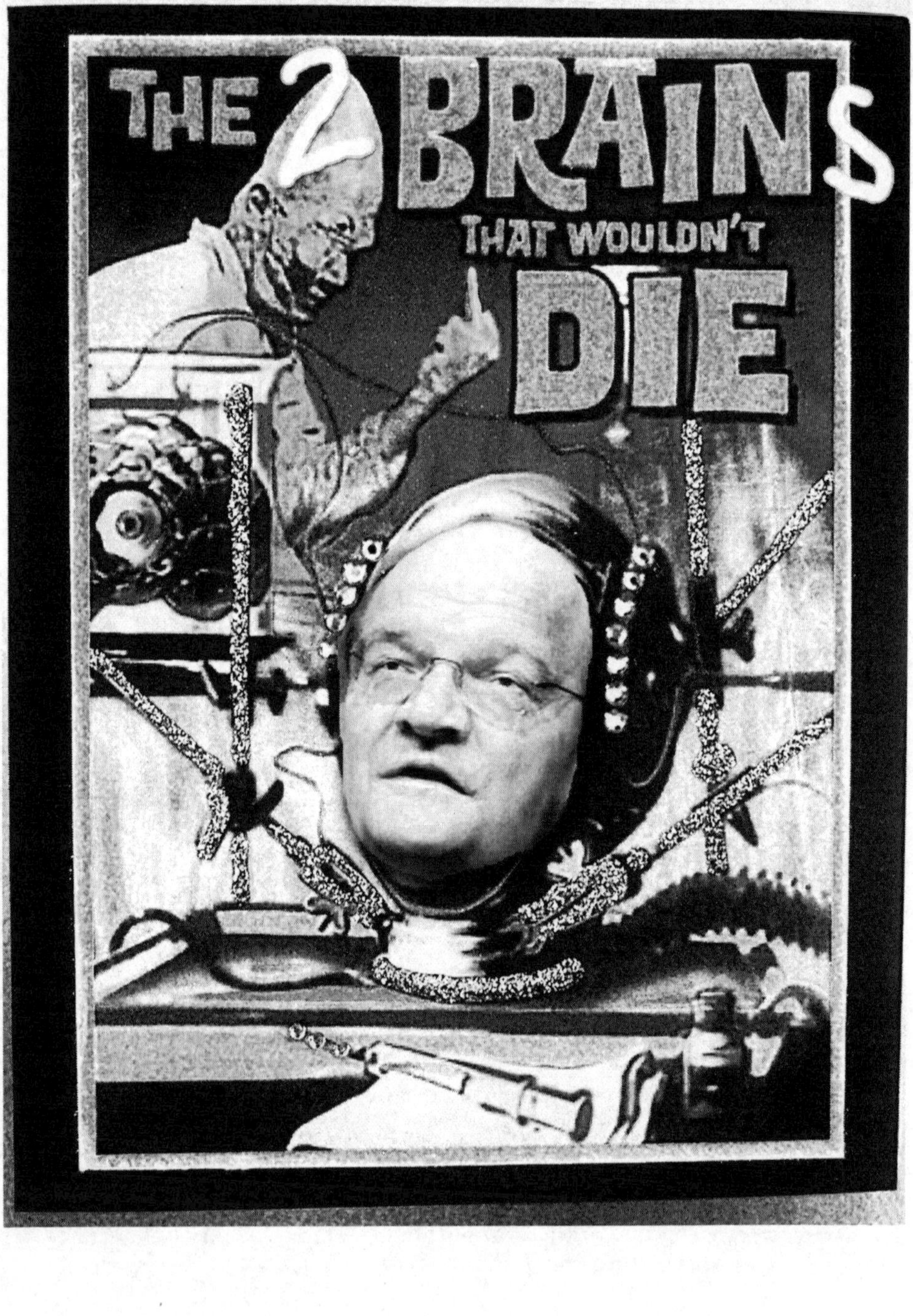
THE 2 BRAINS
THAT WOULDN'T
DIE

families. It's often frustrating to see peaceful marches and reports of community need ignored, and yet political power sits up and takes notice,throwing money and authoritarian measures at a problem, when we witness the spectacular violence of broken windows or burning shops.

Never be alone or anonymous at demonstrations. Take 4 or 5 friends: you can support each other, you can organise help if someone gets arrested or hurt, and it's more fun. It is important to trust each other to speak about how far you want to go and where your personal constraints are - militancy is no competition for the hardest girl/guy. If you judge you want to enter the sort of situation where 'illegal' actions like fights with the police or the deconstruction of banks are likely to take place it is crucial to be masked. In the recent demonstrations in the UK the police were able to arrest people long after the actual events because they had detailed pictures of them. Take surveillance in urban areas as a given. It is often also helpful to have clothes to change into. Be careful with electronic communication in general. Also, be careful when you leave the demonstration, police like to arrest people the moment they are separated from the crowd.

Good planning is very important, especially for direct action in small groups but also for actions within a demonstration. You should know the scenery, be mobile and create events which cannot be foreseen by the police. This is the beauty of militancy: for once it is you who acts and decides where things happen. It can be a very liberating experience of collectively reclaiming political agency. It's the police who have to defend all those banks, supermarkets, government buildings - well the whole unbearable capitalist normality. Make it dance. Be careful, support each other and get going.

Redirecting the action.

Our generation has been raised under the categorical dogma of peaceful protests: we have been force-fed the notion that protests are only legitimate if they are non-violent; the recurring examples of MLK and Gandhi have, ironically, been uprooted from their original radicalism to a universally-shared consensus of exemplary legitimacy. In reality, these figures have been misappropriated by the mainstream political spectrum from left to right, to serve the very system that they fought against. Whether at G20 meetings, WTO rounds or national protests against neoliberal legislation, the media invariably presents to us the same scenario: the approved, responsible citizens marching with discipline ("peace") from point A to point B, right on schedule, and the anomalies: those who take the X trajectory too fast to be monitored and too effectively to be innocuous.

We have internalized this structure: the good protestors and the bad ones. The legitimate and the toxic. We have learned the reflex of deploring the "incidents", the "unfortunate" broken windows, unauthorized gatherings and "barbarically" burnt police vans: "if only the bad apples understood violence is Not the Way!" we exclaim, shaking our heads in condescending compassion. Now we have learnt: protest must remain a performance and never become a threat.

Seven years ago, two million stalked the streets of London, in this very same mode of 'place A to place B' to prevent the slaughter and maiming of a generation of Iraqis for corporate profit, in the greatest mobilisation and failure of mobilisation witnessed in our times. In this perspective, we see that 'peaceful' has become the code word for 'ineffective'. 'Violence', thus, becomes whatever actually disrupts. When 'disruption' means 'violence', 'terrorism' is never very far away. After the modern fear of civil unrest and political upheaval contained in the notion of violence has been invoked, a more contemporary fear of global terrorism has come to invade our collective imaginaries.

Thus 'terrorism' comes to epitomize the ultimate violence, in opposition to which 'simple-plain' war can swiftly take the name of 'peace.' Similarly, any attempt at protest is disavowed by the political and media establishment as illegitimate before it inevitably crosses the path forbidden to it by the all-pervasive discourse of violence. It is this notion of 'violence' that expressly condemns any possibility of radical action against the state. In reality the question of pacifism is serious only for those who have the ability to open fire.

Squatting.

A student loan can be very handy. Most of us need one to help pay for tuition and the increasing cost of living. A top student will want to have all the time they need in a week available for serious study. They will not want to be working a crap job serving coffee to people who probably went to university for free. But let's be honest, the more dosh we have to spend on fees, food and shelter, the less we have to spend on the other things we enjoy in life.

Unfortunately, when it comes to housing, students are cursed with two problems. First of all it's very expensive to rent. If you are thinking of studying in London this is a serious issue and one that has sadly prevented some students from access to the capital. The second problem is exploitative student landlords. This one is a national problem and one that many have fallen foul of. Make no mistake, many landlords out there are crooks, and students, often dealing with these issues for the first time in their lives, are easy pickings. Ideally these landlords would be chased out of town and their offices burnt to the ground by an angry Molotov wielding mob. In practice, petrol is expensive and molotovs may not be cost effective. Instead a better tactic might be to avoid landlords.

Who wants to pay rent anyway? Despite newspaper scare stories, most people who squat are not anti-social layabouts who are happy to take other people's homes. There are a vast number of unoccupied residences, commercial properties, and, forgotten brown-field sites just waiting to have a group of proactive students turn them into homes. Some may say squatters are immoral free-loading scum-bags. That's absolutely fine. Some people also vote Tory and conveniently ignore the contradiction of a housing crisis with vast numbers of potential homes sitting empty (often deliberately), the negligence of councils to house people in their empty properties, the exploitation by property developers, and, the benefits of bringing an unused building back into use for yourself and the community.

Opening your first squat can be daunting and it might not go smoothly at first. There are many groups and networks who have extensive knowledge and resources to help squatters. They are easy to find and have been tirelessly supporting vulnerable people for years (all for no financial return so if you can, support them). Find other groups out there, make use of them, and offer your support when it's needed. Become part of a network, you'll be surprised how important it is to have others to call for help if things get tricky. This could be as simple as borrowing a spanner or resisting illegal evictions from over-excited security companies.

Advice and experience will give you the confidence to have a go yourself. But squatting is a DIY activity and if you and your mates don't know how utilities in a building work you might not get running water or electricity. If you are going to squat you will have to put some work in. That means spending some time hunting for empties and swotting up on fixing up a building and making it secure. The Internet is a good starting point for advice but here are a few practical steps.

- Find a building and ask yourself the following. How long has it been empty and who owns it? In general long-term entries are better. The Council often leave buildings for years and are sometimes slow to evict whilst private owners are unpredictable. Property developers are greedy and rich so coughing up £1200 for a speedy eviction Interim Possession Order is easy for them. That doesn't mean you shouldn't go for it. Property development companies have destroyed the architectural heritage of the country while systematically obliterating communities everywhere - they must be stopped. Consider purchasing the land registry online to discover who the owner is. Are there any planning proposals for the site (check local council planning documents available online)? Is there a way in without causing criminal damage? What are the chances of someone calling the police during entry?

- Read up on the law. It sounds ridiculous but many police don't know the law. That's why some squats choose to put up Section 6 notices to remind Plod that if they smash in your door and kick you out it is a criminal offence. If you get into a situation where they show up and give you hassle, stay calm and reel off your extensive knowledge of property law. Don't open the door and explain this is your home. If you have secured the building, changed the locks and brought it under your control then you are legally squatting and can only be legally removed through the courts. Eventually they'll get bored or confused and leave. Be aware though, entering and securing a building is dangerous because if seen or caught in the act you could be arrested and charged with Criminal Damage, Burglary or even if you haven't done anything yet but have tools, Going Equipped to cause Criminal Damage. Don't get caught in the act of entering. And remember, entering and occupying an unused building is legal but causing damage to enter is not. It's best to keep someone in the building at all times - a reason many squat groups are large enough for this not to be a problem. If the owners come back to an empty building, you are not occupying it and can therefore easily lose it.

if its
BROWNE
flush it
DOWNE
STUDENT MOVEMENTS

- Getting friendly with the neighbours is important too. Many people are sympathetic and it is not uncommon for squatters to get local support. Others will dislike you – often out of prejudice but don't panic. Few change their opinions overnight so a "fuck-you" attitude won't get you very far.

Squatting is time consuming and tiring, plus, it can be socially demanding living with others in non-compartmentalised spaces. But ultimately squatting can be hugely rewarding for your own housing needs but also for the needs of others. Space everywhere is being enclosed. Squats can open it back up. Consider how you might use a space. Could groups from your Uni use a space for something? Putting on events, allowing groups to meet and organise there, or even just offering a place for people to hang together can all create a sense of belonging and social value that no business can match. Space is precious so cherish and use it.

Crime, Episode 4: Ruth Rendell's Miami Vice (chancellor) in the Naked City

Ruth's a second year drama student, but her big vice is that she's lazy, she can't get her act together essay-wise, particularly this latest one on gritty situationist detective series, *the Naked City*. Luckily for her, all the way from Miami is good old Agatha Christie, essay writer for hire. Christie, like her athletic namesake has no qualms about cheating and luckily for her this means she rakes in the cash come deadline day. Realising that her own essays were of passable quality she found that it made sense to offer her 'editing' and 'study support' skills to the posher, richer kids at college. She advertised at Uni and used one of those online services pairing up those hopeless writers with the semi-English literate who mastered the magic formula of writing a half-decent 4000-word tirade... It was fine, only the first and last paragraphs (or pages, if she was really (un)lucky) actually ever got read. Now Ruth is happy and Christie can fulfil some stereotypes with that extra wad for her lunchbox.

Degrees.

Oh precious piece of paper this. Floats above and ahead, a degree, a diploma, whatever one is after. Perhaps there's a purpose behind it – engaging subject matter maybe, a lack of other options, prospect of possible entrance into intriguing or lucrative career perhaps, whatever. The purpose and ideals behind university study are entirely irrelevant to how the education factory functions. No doubt there's a parade of bloated fools in the distance telling you about what you should be doing with your studies – learn this or that, do this or that. To hell with these bores. The one crucial thing they all overlook about this piece of paper is that it is a piece of paper. Filigree font on thick watermark is cute of course, but if you're dreaming through your studies about all the doors this certificate will open, then prepare for a vicious hangover.

The university as it stands is a qualifications factory tightly enmeshed into financial capitalism and its greasy advocates in the British government. Beyond the marketing and careers spiel, the qualifications factory expects you to perform as a customer, though not quite in the way you'd suspect. You're studying at university then? Nice. If you are fortunate enough to actually enjoy the subject matter of your degree, great. Ideals or no, it won't matter either if you're interested in self-development or an easy life. The qualifications factory expects you to quietly and passively chew down your qualification with a requisite mediocre diligence – emulate the established knowledge, copy your teacher, meet deadlines, work alone. In exchange: a piece of paper, a fairly common degree and a reference from a lecturer mediocre enough to strut into a social care or service-sector job. As the customer, you've paid about 40 years worth of future wages in debt in exchange for this piece of paper, so proper behaviour is no doubt in order. You may love your subject and give it all your heart and guts but know that this is a sausage factory where hard work won't be reflected in marking, and any high scores will be converted into prospectus photoshoots and font-size 40 quotations.

The actual customer in the sausage factory however is not you or your piece of paper, however many sleepless nights or panic attacks it demanded. The qualification factory churns out tens of thousands of students with similar degrees in similar subjects annually, reaching a net turnover of high quality butchers' sausages for mediocre employment in the service-sector or the typical graduate employers like marketing, advertising and recruitment. Perhaps this was the end all along. *If you can't beat em, join em - money makes the world go round* - the clichés are familiar and easily recited when you work and sweat off that debt, but the aim of the university and government is to create a large mediocre labour pool to fill its vacancies. Disillusioning? No not really. Only if you're content with settling into a contract where you're the losing party.

The university-factory sells you a degree at the price of the future. The debt now involved in study will take decades of future labour to repay: £27k in average fees as of 2012, will rise again no doubt + personal debts of around £40k+ for high urban rents, living costs plus the spells of inevitable unemployment after graduation. This is a new feudalism for educated young workers, as the future itself is colonised by financial capitalism. When a degree will just about obtain work in a supermarket, nightclub, care-home or casual labouring, workers must surrender 40 years of earnings in order to work for a piece of paper that is now simply a work permit and a piece of cursory cultural capital. Either that or change names, switch cards, being limited by border agencies and ever-avoid creditors ad infinitum. The government doesn't expect this debt to be repaid either, but expects all tax-payers to remain in debt, like itself, and therefore bound to financial institutions, who have caused the economic crisis which is everyday capitalism. Financial institutions donate to political parties, NGOs, purchase media outlets and so on, generally distorting the political process in their favour.

So this piece of paper we've been eyeing in the distance: what to do with it? Like all symbolic pieces of paper - marriage certificates, passports, visas, national insurance number, the degree can be obtained dubiously elsewhere (search Instant Degrees - the question of ideals or purpose for a piece of paper is truly irrelevant to the process of degree obtainment and forgery, as employers will never ask for degree certificates, that piece of paper you so desired). Yet these are symbolically and politically powerful documents, as identity theft or impersonation will reveal. You trade future earnings in exchange for debt, in a contract that returns work or a sense of self-nourishment -- students are customers in the qualifications factory after all. Both we know are irrelevant to the university process. Time comes to make the best of a dreary situation. Tesco degrees, philosophy postgrad funding or project management paid positions won't exist during the inevitable collapse of the labour market in the West, as financial capitalism continues to cut down its HR costs.

There are no bad words for those who take the easy option or the idealistic option. Good and bad are playground games. You're studying at university? Nice. Given the collapse of your future into a debt shitwave, and the honest impossibility of getting a meaningful job that matches up to your course of study, come then get together and do something about it eh? A sausage factory is powered by the soft hands of its workers, their hearts, guts, and other tripe. Get together with others and work out a real solution to the mess ahead. If you can earn a degree and live a life that exposes the fraud of that degree and the fraud of the labour market, then you may well be exactly the kind of people we require. Three years is a long time. Nothing less is at stake than the future itself.

Overqualified, Overworked and Un(der)paid - An Internshipping Forecast.

> When you send something by ship it's called cargo. When you send something by car it's called shipment. When you send someone to fetch you a coffee it's called an internship.

Unpaid internships are illegal. All corporate entities are legally bound to comply with the national minimum wage legislation. This does not apply to not-for-profit organisations (even though many companies, such as Serco, profit off volunteer work), hence the practice of politicians not paying their staff. The other loophole is that you may be unpaid if it's part of a course placement.

For the past two decades the employability of graduates has been integral to government agendas, with universities addressing the issue via curricula and course design. But in the prevailing economic conditions you might already be worried about your future and post-graduation chances of getting a job in order to support and sustain yourself. As such you might have chosen a degree that incorporates a practical element - a work placement, an internship, or whatever they want to call it - supposedly designed to give you a better chance of getting a job, especially if you've never worked in a given profession before. It is understandable why most people believe that a university degree, particularly one that teaches some actual skills wanted by employers, could feasibly be a foot on the first step of the so-called career ladder. It is indeed true that some employers expect applicants to already have a number of placements under their belt, even when applying for their first, entry-level jobs. But still - what is practical? What are proper skills? What is work? Who are these future employers? What even is a career? What career do you want?

The debate around unpaid internships generally centres on social mobility and the fact that for those from unprivileged backgrounds such opportunities remain a closed game. Comments from our local (j)anus-faced, neo-Thatcherite double-act illustrate the divisions and hypocrisy at the heart of the problem. Tory prime minister, David Cameron and his Lib-Dem deputy, Nick Clegg - or should that be the PM's office intern? - have been amongst those mouthing off, but also represent those for whom private wealth meant never worrying about such things. Just as Clegg criticised the idea of 'unpaid internships which favour the wealthy and well-connected', announcing a new scheme promoting the maxim of 'what you know, not who you know' (whilst trashing university education for the poor and having taken lucrative advantage of such opportunities himself), the PM candidly announced that he was fine with the idea of giving internships to the progeny of his friends and neighbours. He said he was 'quite relaxed' about the whole thing. If he relaxes any further his heart may actually stop. No bad thing, you might speculate, but even so, you may realise that in light of this, you're more than likely to be under pressure to complete some unpaid internships yourself post- (or pre-) graduation.

Unfortunately, last year's graduates are fighting for or already juggling a couple of such internships alongside one or two precarious and intermittent jobs. And let's not forget the attendant denigration of conditions – unpaid labour is a way to circumnavigate other employment laws in place to protect workers. What used to be, in the 'good old days' of job availability and stability, useful on-the-job training leading to a permanent position is nowadays often spoken of as a necessary condition of getting paid work, or even 'modern day slavery'. That might sound a bit excessive, but that it is exploitative is beyond doubt. Legislation exists. Enforcement, however, does not appear forthcoming. Mainstream politics is in thrall to the very interests whose furtherance would least be served by the ending of a culture of cheap, disposable labour.

Whilst individual institutions are clearly part of a far wider economic reality, they cannot absolve themselves from responsibility - on the other hand neither can you. You, too, are accepting the situation and undercutting fellow workers. Previously when labourers were (often literally) two a penny, unions and collectives were formed in order to combat just such a situation. This solution seems remote however, within our own diffuse, individualised reality. It is hard to imagine the unionisation of interns within such a competitive and unstable framework.

And so, if hopes of solidarity and enforcement fail, with the traditional weapons of the left undermined in the face of the new neoliberal hegemony, where do we turn for relief from such inherently unjust exploitation? Perhaps we are complicit in our own exploitation, hailed by the dominating ideology. But at least if we can perceive the forces in operation we have a hope of, if not changing them, at least supplanting their pre-eminence within our experiences. If we accept that institutionalised unpaid labour exploits us, we might attempt to move our thinking beyond the reproduction of consensus and an existing ethical or knowledge framework with its inherent transmission of norms of behaviour.

Being hired without conventional employment conditions also allows new behaviours more latitude. We might operate in a sphere beyond the ethical normative bonds that conventionally tie employee and employer. If employers have no consideration for ethical responsibilities then there is likewise no obligation upon 'employees' either. Those of us that find ourselves in the position of being exploited may discover those methods by which we might fight back. This fightback may take the form of a counter-exploitation, worked towards with all guile and determination. Experiences might be maximised for their links to spheres of experience hitherto unreachable, their connections exploited, the knowledge that they purport to convey, stored and turned against itself. Counter-knowledge used against the discourse that suppresses it. The intern can become the agent of psychic leaks, disseminating the unconscious of the organisation beyond its boundaries. They can be the weak link in the organisation's chain, the porous boundary that opens it up to the collective sphere of wider social practice that it, by definition, excludes or captures, setting boundaries to enclose and exploit or else exclude and suppress. Interns can be a virus that infiltrates the heart of such complex systems; they can, through their very porosity and covert refusal of allegiance, affect a larger context by making the exploitation of unpaid labour no longer a viable option for organisations seeking to shield themselves from such subversive practices.

But what of a placement that you are instructed to carry out as part of your course? If you end up working for little, or nothing, in return for something called a 'work experience placement', you might as well try to make the most of it, right? ("And what makes you think you are the right person for this unpaid internship?"... "Well, sir, I acquired years of experience in unpaid internships during my course of study.") Despite all your tutor's good intentions however, you may still find yourself stuffing envelopes in the backroom office, fetching lunch, or maybe even coffee.

Even if you are suspicious of the very idea of time away from lectures or other uni-based activities (organising, activism, reading groups or conferences) in order to work for someone, often full-time, for free, it can have its benefits. Choose an organisation that is fucking with things. You can be a spy and a heretic. You can document their ideologies and their agendas, their intimate dealings, straight from the horses' mouths. Act impressionable. Write down quotes. And if you see any companies publicly advertising for a full-time, unpaid internship, ring them up and threaten to report them to https://payandworkrights.direct.gov.uk/complaints - the 'Pay and Work Rights' government website - then see how long the ad stays up.

COURAGE

Work it.

There once was a story of a girl and a boy who wanted to learn many, many things and grow up with lots of witty and exciting friends, possibly even have a stimulating and reasonably well-paid job in some glamorous metropolitan location. They wanted to understand what the world was about, and have fun, possibly even be happy, just like the shiny acne-free diagrams the career advisor showed them. The name 'university' was surrounded by radiant pearly lights, with the good people of the future offering all kinds of enticing rewards for three years of diligence and dipsomania.

After careful consideration of local McJobs or of three years of expensive university study, a decision was finally made – and for many like the girl and the boy, the first chance of moving away, a room of one's own. But when the euphoria of Freshers and the first year of study wore off, a horrible debt hangover kicked in and made the girl and boy very sad. "Everything is too expensive!", they cried. "There's scarcely enough money to pay rising rents and food! And all this debt for a course that is so confusing, so hard to learn anything from. What on earth are we to do?"

One day when the girl and boy were carrying out an elaborate exchange of character assassinations and snipes over subsidised-cider in the SU bar, a shrunken, shambling and withered figure of grotesque aspect slithered over towards their messy table. The wretched figure seemed familiar. Once it stepped towards the neon-glare of the screen above the table, repeating rolling Hollyoaks/MTV shite, it now appeared to be the Warden, who also happened to be the head of the Publicity, PR and Corporate Handshake office of the university. The appalling man creaked his wizened head towards our hapless pair, and with fetid breath and overbearing frame, slowly whispered, "Why do you wail and cry, my children?".

"We have no money, and our debts will take several lifetimes to repay, sir", the girl replied. "Listen to me, child", said the vile warden, plunging his long dirty nails into his grubby trouser pockets and furiously jangling some unknown chain. "The only way you can make your degree *work for you*", and suddenly his voice sounded almost juvenile, and his face appeared for a second almost youthful, aside from the lines and furrows above his brow, "and be attractive to corporate talent head-hunters, is to work for free. We have links with leading PFI call-centres, nationwide retailers and asset repossession firms. Become an intern for one of these firms, or for Tesco, or Reebok, or the Lib-Dems. You'll never work in your life otherwise." Removing his greasy yellow fingers from his pockets, the warden now turned to the boy, and started poking him rather fiercely in the shoulder. "If not, my child, you'll never have a *proper job* in your life, and then you'll never repay that six-figure debt!" And with that, the vile creature stole away, laughing manically, and began stuffing student pennies into a fruit machine entitled "Knowledge and Creative Industries Corporate Development Consultancies". The machine did not appear to be paying out that night.

The girl and boy followed the wizened warden's advice, but six months on they had even less money, had maxed out their overdrafts, and now their grades were getting worse and worse. They were sincere, they smiled on cue, and they picked up the discarded coffee cups after arrogant art gallery managers and brought coffee for Giles, Seb and Tabitha at the KOOL KREATIVE IT firms they interned at. But those bright colours that cascaded inside their dreams at first were now turning grey. What could they do?

"Very well!" announced the girl, after another dreary evening with the boy exhaustively analysing each other's failings and unfortunate habits over cheap beer. "If we're going to keep paying for ourselves, we'll have to work for actual pay! Whatever it takes!".

As if by magic, the girl and boy stopped reading their books, and started to make some money. After abandoning his erstwhile chums after some ludicrous falling-out, the boy continued to refresh himself in a city-centre hotel bar. A gentleman befriended him and continued to buy him drink after drink. "What a friendly chap!", thought the boy. He later surprised the gentleman in his hotel room with his "so....fucking....good!" technique for massaging particular parts of the anatomy with particular parts of his anatomy. With £20 in his hand, and a phone number to call again next week, the boy began meeting with older gentlemen and "cheering them up" in his own special and profitable way. Soon sugar daddies were buying him dinner, smart clothes, household appliances, textbooks.

Meanwhile the girl, inspired by the boy's entrepreneurial go-getting ability, tried adult modelling, but was having little success. "Do I really have such an awful body?" she wailed, after a particularly successful indie porn site turned down her portfolio. "No, no my child" cried a vile little gentleman of uncannily similar aspect to the warden. "I'll give you some cash, all you've got to do is take your clothes off". He began rubbing his greasy hands together. "Rude photos, you know. A bit *blue*. No pressure". Next term's fees weren't going to pay themselves. Later she and the other model were given lots to drink, and after various aggressive prompts by the photographer and his 'film team', began performing in films and online live-streams like a pro. "At least I'm getting paid", thought the girl. Both the girl and boy felt quite sore and tired, and argued more and more, but at least now they could afford to study, pay the rent and go through the internships mill. And with that, the girl and the boy entered the humiliating world of paid work. And they lived not-so-happily after.

Benefits.

Dirty fackin scroungers, spongers, lazy, feckless and reckless. What once was a matter of entitlement and social support now takes on the colour and language of criminalisation. Welfare is a political issue and a social right, and postgrad and part-time students should look into any jobseeker's allowance or housing benefit they may be entitled to. But signing-on is made as difficult and degrading as possible by endless corridors of constipated bureaucracy demanding the filling out of form X for form Y, or making you have to sign off and sign back on just for a bit of shitty part-time work. Whilst social support is absolutely essential and integral to a just society, successive governments have tried their best to destroy it, leaving what remains creaking and wounded. Learn how to fuck with this spiteful and embittered system.

At the time of writing, you are allowed to do up to 16 hours study per week while claiming jobseeker's allowance. While on jobseeker's, you are also eligible for housing benefit. JSA offers a fixed rate (increasing with inflation) of around about £67.50 per week, if you are over 25. Under 25s get about £14 less (to discourage young people from becoming dependent on welfare, and to force them into shitty minimum-wage jobs – youth NMW being set at a lower rate). This is a passable substitute for a scholarship or a grant, and should be taken up wherever possible with pride and cunning. Don't beat yourself up with their rhetoric, your £53 cannot compare to the multi-million pound tax brakes afforded to millionaires or the cash spilt on horrendous warmongering.

Regardless of how you justify it to yourself, you'll probably need more polished answers for the jobcentre who will undoubtedly hassle you over how many jobs you've applied for. The clerks probably couldn't give a shit but they're beholden to a panoply of disgraceful political targets, threatened or cajoled into enforcing punishments over various petty administrative errors. These same clerks are often faced with the sack not only if they fail to meet vindictive targets, but also if they spend too much time with a "client" or if they even seem too helpful. Depression kicks in. Yet there are no longer any jobs. The staff know this, all you've got to do is pretend and consent to the process – just feed them a plausible story, tell them about hours spent poring over Gumtree or Guardianjobs.

The direct personal experience of signing on forces a confrontation of what would otherwise be mere concepts of ideology and class. There's a conflict between, on the one hand, social guilt and, on the other, resolutely defending the social investment in a professional education that, for some reason, the current neoliberal government doesn't see the value in. Fighting daily against the ideology of work will wear you down, but understand that this is part of the violence of capitalism that is punishing the poor. Don't be beaten, be cheeky.

Be careful whether to inform the jobcentre you are studying for a part-time MA/PhD. They will have to pass a verdict on the validity of this arrangement, which will no doubt be final. If you choose to withhold this information, you may be accused of fraud. In general, when claiming benefits, try to be as outwardly obedient and cooperative as possible; ask questions (about training, CVs, application forms) - you won't get any useful advice, and you may get sent on a soul-destroying course, but it will impress the "decision makers" and keep you off the warning system for punishment. Fill your jobseekers' diary with all sorts of nonsense about looking in the papers, asking around, whatever. If the spectre of New Deal is looming, consider signing off and signing back on. Whatever you do, use what's available and be cunning. Welfare is increasingly used as a form of social punishment but make use of it, play their games, talk their talk and know the entire violence and absurdity of this arrangement.

Crime, Episode 5: Yes Minister, Yes Officer, Professor's Plums in the Library with the Duck House.

The right honourable 'Dave', whilst studying for a PPE degree at Oxford learns that looting lies at the heart of these fair lands, whether the swag be continents, food supplies, philosophies and entire peoples, or oil supplies, aid funds, elections and wages. In fact, his ancestors have perfected the practice to a well-honed art, plundering, snatching, grabbing, pilfering, embezzling, liberating, pinching. But its not just the aristocrats at it, he learns from his textbooks, everyone is doing it! You may be an MP in real need of a duck island and a second home, a Barclay's CEO claiming your employees income tax as your own corporate tax, or a purely criminal ten year old looting buns from Greggs. In a world that defines madness as bucking the trend he speculates, you'd have to be insane not to get in on the action.

So one night at the supermarket Dave gets his good friend Gideon and one of those handy half-trolleys and heads for the checkout. After collecting his items he decides hell, there's a few commodities he doesn't feel like paying for, it is his birthright after all. Dave likes self-checkout, it makes him feel like he's working for once. Gideon tells him it's best not to go for alcohol or large meat – they have tags. Making sure G. knows which items he's after, Dave fills one bag, then puts it in the trolley to make room for the other bags to be filled. As the pair fill the 2nd or 3rd bag, Dave takes a bit of not-yet swag, makes a 'failed' attempt at swiping it, then hands it to Gideon to put in the 1st bag, placed away from the alarming judgement of the scales. The booty bypasses detection and liberates itself from theft as private property.

Dave, keen to keep the mines running, often buys himself a nice, fat bag of coal. He likes to put it in front of him at the self-checkout, then simply pick it up when he leaves. If anything goes wrong he just pleads forgetfulness and technological retardation. An eminently believable defence in his case. He doesn't look around guiltily, no point in getting too big for your (riding) boots, he thinks. If he's ever feeling especially nervous then he knows it's better to back out. Speaking of boots, Dave's friend Sam knows that make-up is pretty easy to burglarise - usually she just sticks it up her sleeves and leaves. Of course, she's a pro. She knows that many items have a small, slightly raised barcode tag, which may set off an alarm. But she also knows that in the more high-end facepaint emporiums (where she is far too common to shop, of course) only the testers are easy to get - so she can work on her immune system too.

Stung by recent critiques, Dave's pal Gideon decides to requisition stolen goods from Sir Pip Green's non-taxed empire. He takes a higher number of clothes into the changing room than the number on the card they give him by having the clothes bunched together, with a bra (sexy "skin" coloured, just the way Davey likes it), hooked on another item, or a top under his arm. If this is noticed it's no big deal – it was accidental, he claims. Now that I have seven items in here, he thinks, I pilfer one. He doesn't even go for the hidden one as he knows that a different person collects the discards. The kinky lingerie he chooses fits snugly under his clothes, and he is careful to remove the tag. He holds the fabric around the tag and pulls the tag until there's a hole large enough to pull the tag through. Luckily, he always carries his nail scissors in his bag, just in case there are some more necessary cuts. He puts the tag in the pocket of one of the items he doesn't want, tidies up the clothes and hands the un-nabbable ones to the courteous worker. He exits quickly but unsuspiciously, listening to Rod Stewart singing 'The First Cut is the Deepest' on his headphones as he leaves the shop, just in case anyone shouts, "Stop! Thief!"

International students.

Schools, now more than ever, need international students to balance their books. This doesn't mean we are treated well. We have money they need, but we are foreign, suspicious, up to no good. The government must balance its desire to make up the shortfall in funding, with its desire to pander to racists and to stay in-line with its own structural racism without contradicting its politics of fear. International students are guilty on arrival... As well as being cash-cows and racialised scape-goats, we are also guinea pigs. New ways of fucking students are tried on us first, as it's difficult to sustain long-term campaigns in support of such a transient group.

The points-based visa system was introduced across UK universities in 2009, and imposed a series of requirements for non-EU students and academics coming to study or teach in the UK - known as a 'Tier 4' visa. New requirements include:

*A demand that students prove maintenance funds (up to £7200 for a one year masters in London);
*Provision of biometric details;
*A licensing system for all educational institutions that wish to accept international students, leading to the vetting of educational institutions by the UK Border Agency (UKBA) and Home Office;
*Monitoring duties imposed on all higher education institutions, including monitoring foreign student and staff attendance.

On top of this, visa applicants may have to: supply birth certificates if they need to use their parent's bank account as a guarantor (for those of us who don't have 7000 in our accounts), have the bank manager sign every page, and, of course, prove that we can speak English (as if the application process isn't hard enough to decipher).

This has led to a huge increase in late arrivals and no-shows of international students. There is a limited appeals system, so some students have lost thousands of pounds in advance fees, plus visa application fees. 14,000 would-be students were still stuck in Pakistan when term started in October 2009; Students were rejected by the UKBA for a variety of trivial reasons, including having written 'Malaysian' instead of 'Malaysia' under country, or for the colour of the background used in their photograph. At the end of January 2010, the UK Border Agency completely suspended student visa applications from northern India, Nepal and Bangladesh, leaving thousands of potential students stranded.

In January, 56 UK colleges, including many state-funded further education colleges and many other household names, had their licences suspended, meaning that they can no longer invite international students. The colleges, when suspended, were not told of the evidence or allegations against them. While the new points based immigration system definitely goes after university students, the main suspects in town are all the 'other' kinds of international students. Universities are big business, which the government knows. But the small, underfunded colleges are, after all, where the not-so-rich international students end up. Hence the revoked licences and the various 'exposes' and articles about these being merely a front for - you guessed it - Islamic terrorism.

Goldsmiths management last year compiled a list of international students who had not completed a (defunct) online registration process, and threatened to pass this information on to the UK Border Agency. Meanwhile, at Queen Mary, students are rounded up and made to show their passports regularly. After having paid up to £14,000, students are made to feel like criminals - international students reconfigured as terrorist cash-cows.

Staff must check international student attendance. If a student fails to attend 10 'expected interactions' (seminars, lectures, tutor meetings, etc), the professor is obliged to report them to the UKBA. This can lead to deportation in extreme cases. Academics must inform the UKBA if they have any suspicions that a student is breaching the conditions of his or her leave, or if the student is engaging in 'suspicious behaviour'. That monitoring destroys the relationship of trust between academics and students, and threatens the very ethos of academia. By contracting out the work of UKBA to lecturers, these new regulations are turning the university into a site of border control.

Organisations:

*Students NOT Suspects is a campaign in strong opposition to the new visa regulations.
* The Joint Council for the Welfare of Immigrants offers legal representation and runs a rights-based campaign for asylum-seekers.

What you can do:

*Take part in any visa and immigration campaigns around campus, help organise around these issues – international students need support from the wider student body.
*Ask all of your lecturers/tutors if they are monitoring attendance and what they are doing with that information. Refuse to sign any attendance roll if you think it is being passed on to anyone. Pressure your tutors to refuse to comply with UKBA monitoring.
*Wherever you're from, talk to non-EU students about their problems and how they dealt with them. Pass this info on - it could be very useful to someone else.
*Remember that international students are a vital part of any resistance to the corporatisation of higher education. Never buy into antagonisms that may be set up between domestic/EU and 'others'.
*Invite us over for Christmas dinner.

[Facts and figures were nicked from the brilliant Manifesto Club report, 'Fortress Academy' by Valerie Hartwich.]

Plagiarism.

Plagiarism is stealing. Plagiarism is theft. Plagiarism is cheating. Plagiarism is immoral. Plagiarism is done by bad and lazy students. Plagiarism is the nemesis of creative, individual genius. Plagiarism is a crime. Plagiarism is a nuisance to the machinations of the university. Plagiarism is bullshit.

Plagiarism criminalises and covers over a better conversation about sharing, sampling, collusion, collaboration and conspiring. Plagiarism polices the borders of a fictive individual to allow collective thought to be cut into portions, priced and packaged as intellectual property. Plagiarism is one of the poorly paid security guards of private property. Plagiarism discourages people from working together and thinking of study as a collective project. Policed plagiarism allows history to be told in the proper names of singularly great people. Plagiarism is a denial of the way thought and ideas are actually produced. Plagiarism is a dirty name for the system of shared knowledge that we collectively inherit and the collective knowledge production that is supposedly what we do at university. Hard to put a price tag on, though. Precisely where plagiarism steps in with super back-to-school savings on cut-price thought. Everyone does it, just not everyone is punished for it. An argument begins about plagiarism and already repeats someone else. Teachers will be doing it each year, cut-and-pasting the work of PhD and graduate students for their latest summer door-stopper, *Discipline and Publish* by Dr. (students of) Lotti Stash. Newspapers and websites plagiarise the press releases of one or two news-wire agencies. Shit, even tap water has been through countless other people's pipes.

Still, if you get caught plagiarising, it will be a massive fucking hassle. At best they will just fail you on the particular course and put a friendly reminder of your crime against Humanities/Sciences/whatever on your transcript. At worst, they will kick you out of the university and make it difficult for you to get into another one. Cutting and pasting from Wikipedia or lifting paragraphs from a book is reasonably stupid, anyway. If you actually like what you are studying, plagiarism is like shooting yourself in the foot to spite your face. More importantly, it is very likely you will be caught. But, there are perfectly good reasons why you might need to plagiarise, like, for example, having personal issues that your university refuses to acknowledge. You shouldn't have to parade your personal problems in front of a punitive stranger for their judgement if you don't want to. Lying is completely justified in this instance and people are likely to get squeamish and give you an extension or whatever if you talk about something gruesome like genital bleeding or a prolapsed anus. Anyway, if you feel you need to plagiarise, keep the following in mind.

Programs like Turnitin are pretty standard in universities these days. They require you to submit your work online so it can be checked against a massive database of internet sources, published works, and other student essays. (They will then store your essay in a database and make money off it without paying you. This isn't theft or even plagiarism, just 'fair use', apparently.) The exact algorithms they use are kept secret, but it is likely that the main search function works by breaking text into three word sequences. For example, the sentence 'The Tories are the enemy, but Labour are traitors' gets broken down into the following triplets:

The Tories are **Tories are the** **are the enemy**
the enemy but **enemy but Labour**
but Labour are **Labour are Traitors.**

Even when used on a reasonably subject-specific database, like the entire archive of the Financial Times, three word sequences are unique about 70% of the time. It can also detect if you have just added/changed a few words:

The Tories are the enemy and should have theirs heads put on spikes,
but Labour are traitors and war criminals.

So, yeah, even making quite major additions or alterations won't help you much. Turnitin can still make a neat calculation of what percentage of your essay is plagiarised. Even if you use quotation marks but forget to reference due to coffee narcosis, you will probably have to have a reasonably shit conversation with someone staring accusingly at you. If you want to copy something you are going to need to make sure it has never been published in any way, submitted to a program like Turnitin, and never been put online. So, most probably, you are going to have to re-write every sentence in your own words whilst keeping the above in mind.

Anyway, there is a better way. Collusion is the best type of plagiarism. Collusion is secret or illegal cooperation or conspiracy - sounds great, cloak and dagger stuff. For plagiarism though, this means that if you and your friend/friends work on an essay together, then both hand in similar texts, you might be done for plagiarising each other. Bullshit, right? The university puts a ban on the exact type of collective work that should be encouraged. Fuck them, do it. Work with as many people as possible. Organise study groups, discuss each other's essays and work together. Summarise texts for each other, share references, write up sections for each other, use each other's strengths, share arguments. Learning to work together without getting caught by the spotlight of a disciplining regime is definitely the best thing you can learn at university.

Debt.

I answered my door a couple of weeks ago. It was a guy in a black motorcycle helmet with his visor still down. I thought he was there to shoot me. I started thinking about all the stuff I did that week that could get me killed. By the time I got to the letter C on my list he handed me a letter. Made me sign for it. He left without a word and I opened it. It was a notice about a court case, all the way from Middlesex County Court in Boston, Massachusetts. J. Lebowski vs. Harvard University. Fuck, I didn't like my chances. For twenty years they've been asking for their loan back. 10 grand. Now they want 25 for their troubles. Jesus, that was twenty years ago. You'd think they would lose the paperwork by now or something. I've lived all over the goddamned world. How did these bastards find me. Do they really expect their money back after all these years?

After all, there's a lot of stuff people lent to me twenty years ago and I don't have it anymore. Bubba Contreras lent me his Husker Du album. Martha lent me her portable Edgar Allan Poe. Fred lent me his hat. I don't see any of them taking me to court.

I know what you're saying. He should set an example for the students and pay his debts. After all he's a professor. He teaches ethics for Christ's sake. He's bringing the University of London into disrepute. Well, it's not that I don't want to pay them back. It's just that if it were important, they would not be asking for it back. If it were important, I could not pay it back, and they would not take it back, and anyway no one could calculate it. No one could say how much I owe them and how much they owe me, if it were important. If it were important, this debt would be bad.

Because everything that's worth anything to me, anything important, I got from bad debt. I got and I gave, but I never gave back. I never gave back to the creditor. I never gave back to the community. I never gave back what I took, and I never got back what others took from me. They never asked.

And I never would.

Fred taught me why I should give a shit about Shakespeare. Bubba taught me about music. I never gave them anything for this. I don't know what it's worth. It's incalculable. They would never accept anything in exchange. And I went into bad debt with those I loved, a kiss that I could not take back, a look that was never returned.

And out of all this bad debt came connections, not the kind of connection that says oh shit we are all in debt because of capitalism and this should bring us all together. Fuck that. My bad debt, our bad debt already lives beyond capitalism. It doesn't bring us together. It makes us different, again and again. Because nothing equals anything else, and the debt just grows, the connections to all these different bad debts get deeper and deeper, more and more complicit. And when you enter this world of bad debt, this sub-prime undercommons, you are accepted without question, without price, without credit. You enter the house, the family of bad debt, the house that has to keep moving, the fugitive family.

I'm not telling anyone what to do. Sometimes we need money, we need credit, we want credits, we want to graduate. But sometimes we need to study instead, to study together, never graduate, never get credit, never give credit where credit is due, just study together, and get in bad debt to each other, and figure out what's important, figure out what's always different, what's always something else. Just study together til they kick us out, speculate together until they move us along. Kids broke windows and took stuff this summer. They don't plan to give it back. They took what they needed and they took what they wanted and they didn't leave their credit card details. They say these kids were thugs, that they are criminals. Maybe they were, but if being criminal means knowing it's good credit and not bad debt that makes us slaves, then maybe they know something we need to learn. Maybe being in the black means being in the red, and maybe being in the red means being in the black.

Either that or don't open your door.

Law.

We know law as the fixture and measure of relations in a community, be it political, social or economic. Laws have been created to protect the rights of subjects in a state, to determine acceptable social behaviours by punishing those who deviate from them into crime. The bad people break the law and are captured by the police, who then refer a minority onto sentencing by the judiciary, a special class of social and moral experts with funny wigs. The bad people are then punished by time in prison, whilst the police exist to protect the public from violent or corrupt contagions. Law and order as the bleach-mouthwash of the body politic.

It's a nice story, they all are, but stories are for kids and we're done with telling ourselves why we now can't have what we deserve, what generations of our families have fought for - a basic standard of life and meaningful political participation. The majority of laws would exist by social consent. No-one wants to get arrested; a night in the cells is a nasty experience and prisons are horrible, dangerous places. Laws limit our behaviours: a criminal charge undermines getting work, thwarts CRB checks. Law exists in order to control relations and protect the powerful: we know from MPs scandals, bank bailouts and the Bullingdon Club restaurant riots (versus the August 2011 Greggs and Lidl riots) that it's one law for the rich, another law for the exhausted looking man or woman sitting next to you.

Ninety-seven percent of criminal charges are dropped [see Nick Davies' *Flat Earth News*] whilst plenty of prison officers, police and politicians privately admit that the justice and prison system has no obvious deterrent on criminal activities. With the majority of prisoners suffering from mental health, alcohol and substance problems before incarceration, as well as acute social deprivation, law exists to brutally repress more fundamental social problems (and this is something cops we know have told us too). It exists not so solve crime but to "beat anti-social behaviour" as the latest Home Office report puts it, usually with truncheons, bullets, or excessive prison sentences in overcrowded jails. 'Habeas Corpus', the right to be actually charged with a crime when imprisoned, was suspended by the 2005 Prevention of Terrorism Act - similar states of exception and emergency occur elsewhere, demonstrating that law is made and broken in order to oppress and manage social populations. It will not protect you, despite the nicest intentions of police you may know, as a long enough history of institutional racism, violence, failing to respect victims of sexual and domestic violence attest. You don't have to be guilty to be put in prison in this country; in fact you don't even need to be charged. The law sanctifies this corrupt, stinking mass of war, violence and poverty we politely call the status quo. Law is the ether that makes everything fade to black as financial capitalism violently fist-fucks us into a deliriously dire future.

We don't need to fear the law but we cannot trust it either – too many people are in prison for politicised crimes. Whilst MPs, newspaper magnates, business parasites and police cooperate to protect each other's interests in a paranoid game of chicken, we need to keep steady and sensible. The law cannot try a person without a name: remain anonymous, remain legion, and, if arrested, remain silent. You may find it sensible to be selective in your battles – more may be done via systemic letter writing, community activism, symbolic broken windows or website hacking than a fight with a burly cop. Delete personal info (workplaces, identifiable details) of your identity online – keep your Facebook but remove traces, remove emails and messages that might incriminate you or others, such as any statement which might encourage a criminal offence. For those who want to organise illegal actions, which we are not condoning but neither can we condemn, stay sober and be careful. Save a good lawyer's phone number in case of arrest on protests, riots or busts, or the Green and Black Cross legal team [07946 541511], and download and print a bust-card, keeping it on you at all times.

Anxiety is our contemporary condition - a fear of the unknown, a generic fear of indiscernible origin. Psychoanalysis treats anxiety by identifying this repressed cause of fear. Let's be clear about what we're doing, identify what this generic source of anxiety is. Law plunges us into states of despondency, cynicism and passivity, internalising our own submission under the violence of financial capitalism and its inevitable and worsening effects of poverty, anxiety and corruption. Law is a consensus of rights. What of a right to shelter, to political participation, to equal pay and access to employment, to clean water, to communal access to land, to peace? We call on a law-making revolt, spilling out of the school and the universities all those like you, like me entirely enraged. For a future free of debt, war and waged exploitation, by whatever necessary means – that's our law, that's our right.

If you are arrested, remain silent and answer 'no comment' to all questions and interviews until you've had legal advice. Refuse the duty solicitor, however long it will now take. A 'friendly chat' might generate evidence, which contradicts a later and more informed statement. You are entitled to a phone-call, which you should use to contact a friend – instruct them to contact the Green and Black legal team, or a good solicitor. Most arrests won't result in prosecution. Keep calm and keep fucking shit up.

Do it yourself:

Organising.

Money. Debt. Workload. Shit. Doubt. Shit. Deadlines. Shit. Shit. We work together because we have to, we organise together because we need to, sidestepping ten thousand clumsy blows, becoming anonymous, cheeky, fleet-footed, together. First thing: forget whatever you learned about working on your own. Organise the students in your classes or seminar groups. Teachers are increasingly overworked and shouldn't be relied on. Avoid hierarchical groups - set up a reading group, for study, for action, for mad adventures. Doesn't need to be entirely political - the political occurs in being creative, making new, sidestepping power-blocs. Make a blog, a plan, announce at the beginning or end of a class or on a noticeboard. Hijack emailing lists, find spaces, find each other.

Why? Collective intelligences thrive, and informed networks can beat already-existing networks. You know this from the news, from school. Work together against bad decisions or bad teaching by doing it with others. Organise against the organisation, sidestep that same old divide and conquer. We make maps and wander around the grey spaces of the city drinking beer and cursing the gods.

British pond-water

Skip hierarchies: they're boring and generally a time-waster. Uni societies, internship schemes, any kind of unpaid or managed experience - forget it. Do it with others but make it new - collective writing, prank groups, theatres, pirate film making, wild sports, punk bands. Steal into uni offices and rinse out their photocopiers.

Befriend porters, postgrad students, curious types in the local pubs and clubs. People enjoy breaking the rules and doing something unusual, it's an undocumented psychological need, so forget frosty first impressions. Organise a network and be anonymous. University may be just 3 years. There are no magic jobs at the end, unless call-centre tarot counts.

Geeks have dark arts, sucker

Things can fuck up. Essays get written the night before. If you feel like you're the only one panicking, head to the library - you're bound to bump into a classmate compulsively hitting wordcount. Then head to the Psychology section to read up on procrastination. Save money and time by registering on aaaaarg.org and library.nu, and download your books from here. Try other uni libraries or local libraries. Use Amazon's preview and Google Books to take excerpts from books. Find relevant online dictionaries for your subject; they exist. Don't use Wikipedia - seriously. Teachers check, they use it for their own hackneyed journal articles and mediocre chapter entries.

Drowning in a sea of shit

Don't be afraid of debt. The entire Western world is steeped in it. Play the system, borrow as much as you can on the cheap interest rate and have fun. Organise and you won't get caught so easily. Save money by avoiding bad clubs and pubs and having house and squat parties. Brew your own booze. Dumpster-raid when necessary, otherwise steal. But borrow money first and organise your wayward life. Download OpenOffice for free instead of MS Office. Download albums and films for free from Filestube or Vuze. Download trial versions of key software, e.g. Adobe Acrobat or Photoshop and then download keygens so you can use at home after.

The old world is crumbling.

The old world is crumbling, rage is rising, a corrupt elite clings to its swaying gantry, stealing and selling off more and more of our common inheritance. But make no mistake, they are shitting themselves. Privatisation is theft; this parasitical class, like a cornered wild animal, are angry, frightened, desperate and dangerous. Ravenously, they snatch away at our means of living, ever more desperate to maintain their position. By hook or by crook they seek to stem the collapse: militarised policing, ideological attack, all out sell-offs or insidious backdoor stitch-ups, the end result is the same. Yet, as wages fall, as living standards plummet, as our means of survival are outsourced and sold back to us at a profit, we stalk amongst the ruins with an icy glint in our eye. For we know that each new land grab is more desperate than the last, that the infinite expansion this disease so breathlessly chases in order to survive is slipping ever further from its grasp. It will stop at nothing - war, incarceration, impoverishment, the destruction of lives - but this is its undoing. For each new push it makes, we push back stronger. The contradictions are catching up, each new one more immense than the last. The tide that its guardians seek to hold back is rising, and one night, soon, it will surge in through battered down doors and smash the whole sorry charade to pieces.

Every time the system teeters on the precipice, rulers, bankers, the rich, all clutch at straws. Hasty new deferrals are thrown together by the panic stricken princes, hurriedly rushed out from high up in those glittering towers that stab the at sky in the heart of our cities. For a while they struck a deal with us, wages, jobs, homes, property, consumer goods. We, or at least some of us, could live, raise our families, enjoy our lives in peace, health and relative security. But the deal is off. The welfare state has had its heart ripped out by the insatiable greed of those rulers. Never forget that they need to grow, to accumulate more and more, or they will die. Our hopes of home ownership, job security, an education, a healthy, peaceful, fulfilling life, were all ultimately too much for them to stomach. The thought of us prospering without them profiting made them sick to the core. Where were their profits? Their dividends? Their growth? Our hopes and dreams have become little more than a trifling obstacle to their infinite greed, to be bulldozed into the ground with unrelenting brutality.

When we can't afford a house any more, when we don't have a job, we can't afford to fill our homes with pointless tat, iPads and garbage disposal units, when we have nothing to lose, then the debt factory is a busted flush. A new means of controlling us was needed, a new way of instrumentalising and enslaving our passions into their petty and desperate game. Forcing students to pay for their education was a strategy, make no mistake, for creating a lifetime of debt for younger generations. This is not only a guarantee of decades of interest, it is a straitjacket forced upon living, herding us onto 'productive' tracks, less gravy train, more cattle-truck to nowhere. At a basic level they want to entrench their class power. This is the logic of privatisation, or to call it more accurately, the naked and repellent theft of our futures.

So having put the class firmly back into classrooms, marketised our aspirations, de-skilled our schooling, ripped us off at every turn, perhaps we have some questions...

Q - Do students go to university to get a job at the end of it?
A - Yes.

The Labour Force Survey shows unemployment among new graduates at 18.5% (more than double the basic figure across the population). 60% of firms say it makes no difference whether a job candidate has a degree. A poll of financial services, IT, manufacturing and education sectors found that 80% would prefer a school-leaver with three years work experience than a graduate.

These figures do not apply to the students from rich families, who can afford private schooling and top universities. Nearly all managerial positions are reserved for these students. More than 85% of top positions in the government, banks, big companies, media, civil service, etc., are occupied by graduates from a few elite universities such as Oxford and Cambridge.

However, due to low family income and poor quality primary and secondary education, the majority of the lower and even the middle strata of the working class are robbed of the chance of going to the university. Even the upper strata of working class students usually end up in 'second class' universities and subsequently low paid jobs. Status is already determined by class, the old cliché is true: it does not matter what you know, but who you know! Make no mistake, this is a war, fought by them against us; they are panicking, hence their desperate assault on education, rammed through in the teeth of bitter resistance with all necessary violence.

Q - Do students go to university to become independent?
A - Yes, definitely.

A recent report stated that only maths, engineering, law and medicine degrees led to greater lifetime earnings than those of non-graduates. On average the starting salary for a graduate who has done the 'right' course and is lucky to find an office job related to her field of study is £16,000. After tax, national insurance, pension contributions and the graduate loan, the total take home figure is around £1,000 a month.

Obviously, a young graduate who has found a job wishes to become independent. But with this level of income and the average house prices being £160,000, it is impossible to buy even a one bedroom flat, particularly in big cities like London. Banks do not give mortgages more than 3.5 times salary and they ask for 20% down payment, which is impossible for a young graduate to pay.

What about renting? According to the rentright.co.uk the average rental price for a studio flat in September 2011 is £1,047. So we have to borrow £47 a month just to pay the rent and then live on air!

But what is the average monthly living cost for a one bedroom flat? Some cursory research show us figures for Water at £33.50 (not on a meter), Council Tax - £79 (including 25% discount for living alone), Gas - £17, Electric - £26, Phone and Broadband - £25, TV Licence - £12, Food - £100, which comes to the total of £292.50. A figure we have to borrow every month, even before buying stuff to wash ourselves and our old clothes and travel to work to earn.

According to the Office for National Statistics, figures to April 2011 show that the median salary for graduates aged 22-64 was £29,900. Having a degree does not pay off until you are well in your 30s and your income reaches a peak at 51. If you are from the working class but lucky enough to get a degree and find a job, forget about becoming really independent before you are in your 40s.

Q – How much debt will I end up with for doing a degree?
A – A lot.

For full time domestic/EU students starting this year, the yearly Tuition Fee Loan (TFL) is about £3,375 and the Living Cost Loan (LCL) for food, bills, books, travel and accommodation is about £2,906 - a total of £6,281. Thus, your total debt after graduation, before interest, would be £18,843. Because your loan is classed as an income based loan the interest charged would be 1.5% (APR), but this rate most probably increase in near future.

Assuming the interest rate does not change, your total debt (TFL+LCL) after adding the interest accumulated during the 3 years of study will be £19,127. Also, if the average salary for graduates increases on the basis of 4% (the rate of the current rate of inflation), which is unlikely again (because many salaries, particularly in the public sector, have been frozen), and you are lucky to get a job immediately after your graduation on the average salary, then your initial salary will be £17,998 in 2014.

The repayment threshold up to 5 April 2012 will be £15,000 gross each year and repayments will be equal to 9% of any income above the threshold. On the basis of these assumptions, we can now calculate the debt put on your shoulders by the state. This calculation shows that:

- After 10 years of continuously working, the debt balance (£16,559) catches up with the actual debt (£16,314). This means that for the first 10 years we will be paying only the interest on the loan!
- Although the first annual payment comes to £270, it increases to £1,047 in year 11 and £2062 in year 20.
- It takes at least 20 years to clear the debt, if we don't get sacked, inflation remains low, our employer doesn't freeze our salary, the interest rate doesn't increase, etc., etc. With these assumptions, we can finish paying the debt at the age of 41, but pigs might fly too!

Currently, the rate of inflation is claimed to be around 4%. However, their calculations includes the prices of items such as computers, TVs, mobile phones, etc, which are falling continuously, whereas the prices of basic commodities such as food, electricity, water, accommodation, travel etc., are rising all the time. Calculating the rate of inflation for these items shows a figure of 16%, which rapidly eats up the income of a worker. Moreover, with the worldwide food, fuel and housing crises, this situation will likely get even worse.

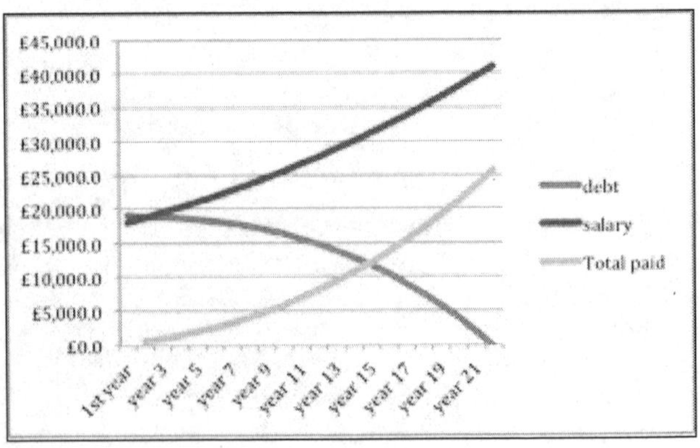

Q - What about starting my degree in 2012?
A - Sorry mate, you are entering a black hole!

As a full-time student starting next year, your yearly Tuition Fee Loan (TFL) is around £9,000 and your Living Cost Loan (LCL) for food, bills, books, travel and accommodation is about £5,187, a total of £14,187. Thus, your total debt after graduation but before calculating interest would be £42,561. Here again for the ease of calculations we assume the interest charged on your loan would remain at 1.5% (APR) for the lifetime of the loan. Is this wishful thinking? Certainly! This rate will probably increase many times during the next decade.

On the basis of the aforementioned assumptions your total debt (TFL+LCL) at graduation will be £45,176. Assuming the state's alleged current rate of inflation (4%) remains unchanged during the lifetime of this debt and you get a job immediately after graduation on an average salary, then your initial salary will be £21,054 in 2014.

The threshold from 2012 will be £21,000 gross each year and repayments will be equal to 9% of any income above the threshold. One the basis of these assumptions we can analyse the experience of being dropped into a financial black hole by the state. The calculation shows that:

- After 20 years of working continuously, the debt balance (£41,755) catches up with the actual debt (£41,141). This means that for the first 20 years we will be paying the interest on the loan!
- Although the first annual payment comes to £4.9, it increases to £1,027 in year 11 and £2,012 in year 20, £3,161 in year 26 and £4,019 in year 30.
- It takes at least 35 years to clear this colossal debt, yet the government states that we have to pay for 30 years only! With our assumptions, this amounts to £49,577 and when we stop repayments we will be 51. More likely we will have to pay this debt until we retire.

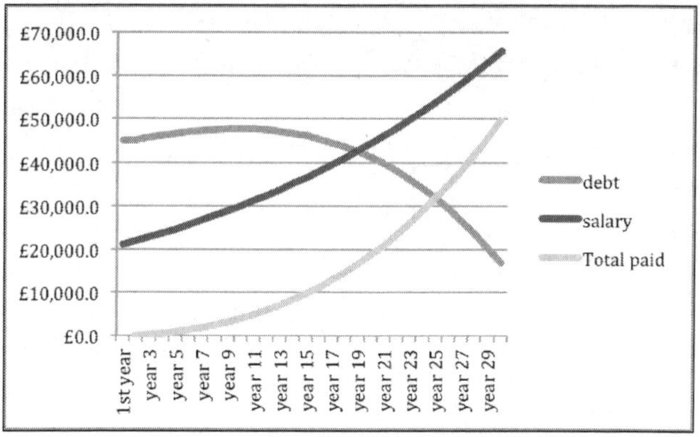

So what are we going to do? Resign ourselves to a best-case scenario of a lifetime of wage slavery? A endless, embittered daily, weekly, yearly struggle to survive, a numbing countdown until you finally retire aged 70 and collapse exhausted into your grave whilst the rich chink champagne flutes on their fifth cruise this year and enjoy their expansive retirement, bought with the fruits of your labour, jet-setting around gated resorts in former and present British colonies? Maybe you will throw in your lot with the literally millions of others already stirring against this immense clusterfuck. There is only one way out of this prison cell, and that is to take it apart brick by brick, wall by wall, tear down the gates, and the towers, and the palaces, and drive the whole sorry cartel out of town. Its not going to be pretty. Remember, politicians, media execs, vice chancellors, the judiciary, bosses, bankers, and their police attack dogs, they are not like you, they will not suffer what you suffer, they will not feel what you feel. Remember therefore, they are out to keep you down, and remember they are shitting themselves.

This is dry and dull

Go beyond the university in ten (and a half) easy steps.

I

The existing university is irredeemably fucked. Education conceived as a discrete object to be acquired, now bought, is the disastrous consequence of not conceiving of it as ongoing, social activity, or practice. The university tries to ignore its foundation as a social activity with a definite history.

The traditional university produces knowledge as distinct from society, and does not consider the production of truth as itself a social, practical and material activity. In conceiving critical knowledge in the abstract, the university denies the place of social, practical and material activity as a mode of critique. The university cannot conceive of itself as a practical-critical activity.

Are students revolutionary? who counts as a student?

No such thing as society. (nothing outside the context)

II

Knowledge cannot be gained outside society, or outside practical everyday life. Truth, being socially constructed, cannot therefore be proved outside of its realisation in social relations.

There is in fact no distinction between the university and "the real world", i.e. work, domesticity, life etc. - this distinction is ideological and tries to hide the possibility of a solidarity between students and workers. In doing so it conceals the realization of 'scholarly' critique through practical, everyday situations and the acknowledgement of the practical contradictions of existing social relations within the university. Students ~~are~~ the revolutionary ~~class~~ of the university. The university and society interpenetrate each other at every point.

what about cleaners? porters?

could be

including those who wish to learn but are excluded by an elitist university system

III

It is essential to educate the educator. The professor should not be respected according to status but only praxis. Until the professor deigns to speak to the student as equal, academic critiques can only be conceived as something to be necessarily overcome in practice.

?? W.T.F.

If the students ever seriously threaten to take over the university, we predict that the overwhelming majority of professors will side with the bureaucratic guardians of the status quo: vice chancellors, wardens, senior management and boards of

Some people want to run things, some things just want to run!

directors. aren't you just instrumentalising in the same kind of way?

IV

The university's pretence to be above the socio-economic reality of society means that it is ill-prepared for the mortal danger it now faces. In seeking to uphold the 'universal' values of 'knowledge' and 'truth', and set these in opposition to the instrumentalised application of thought to economic circumstances it creates a false opposition. The university forgets that its own enlightenment values are fundamentally socially and materially constructed by a historical bourgeoisie through the practical realisation of a critical aim, that aim being the overthrow of the feudal order. Empirical, rational and critical enquiry, conceived as abstract, isolated and specialised activities were the primary weapons of the capitalist class in assailing the palaces of priests and princes.

V

The intellectual class has been historically tolerated and directed by the capitalist owners of production. This class sure up their power and fuel the advances of technology and knowledge required to overcome the inevitable crises and contradictions inherent within the capitalist system. Even the ostensibly anti-capitalist knowledge produced by critical theory operates as a means by which capital can resolve itself in new syntheses. Alongside this, the intellectual is likewise to the capitalist what the priest was to the prince – ideological cover.

This is possible only in as much as the university cannot conceive of itself as integrated into social life. The university must be dissolved into ordinary life in so much as all work must become practical-critical activity. Study cannot be meaningful if it exists only to increase our social capital or our earning potential, and thus to increase the capital of those companies for whom we are forced to apply all of our creativity. The university, until it is collectively owned and run by the students, should be subverted into groups for whom praxis is the production of political consciousness precisely through action and who exploit the ideological framing of the existing university as a 'radical' space, abstracted from society as cover for their activities. Students must organise themselves into "think-tanks" in a ballistic sense so that they leave the university with the power and solidarity to destroy capitalism from the inside.

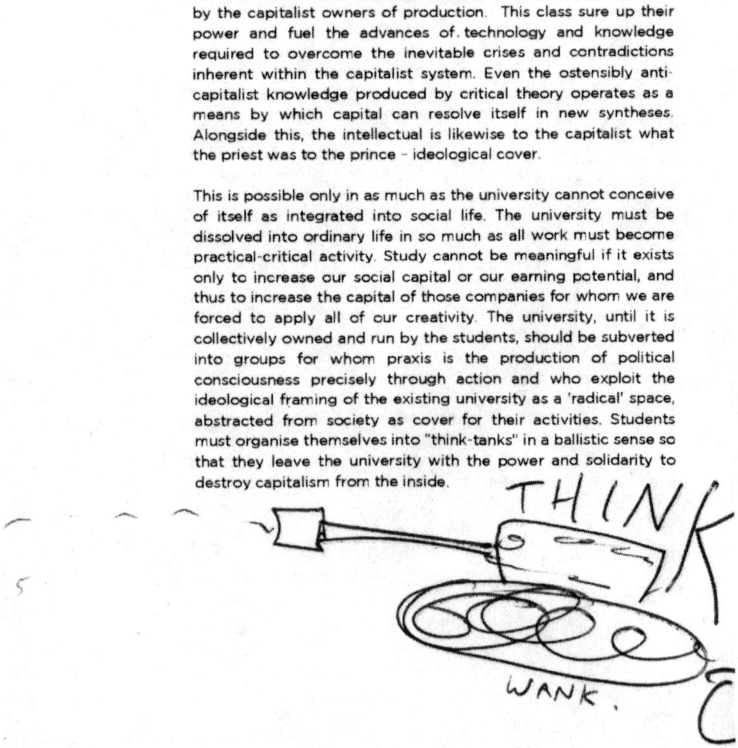

VI

The university resolves the contradictions of capitalist society into abstract knowledge. It now claims that all knowledge and all truths are relative to the individual point of view. In reality, knowledge and truth are the ensemble of social relations.

There is no truth outside society - there is no "objective truth", there is no view from nowhere. But there is also no such thing as "individual truth", i.e. personal, subjective and self-made. Truth and knowledge are socially constructed concepts, which means they have no meaning outside their function within the history of really existing and changing society. In conceiving knowledge as an abstract, universal object or critical tool, rather than a continual process realised through social activity, the University sows the seeds for the alienation of this knowledge from its critical context - and hence for its instrumentalisation by capital. The opposition between capitalist 'knowledge for the sake of personal economic augmentation' vs enlightenment 'knowledge for knowledge's sake' is not truly an opposition at all. There is no such thing as autonomous knowledge. Rather both of these forms of knowledge arise in social relations and historical class conflict and both are masked by the ideology of the class they serve. The only 'true' knowledge therefore, is that which changes historical circumstances themselves and thus proves its own truth in practical, social realisation - knowledge as critical social praxis. All genuinely critical knowledge is therefore revolutionary in the practical sense.

VII

The university cannot see that knowledge is itself a social product because the professors suppose their role to be the pursuit of knowledge for knowledge's sake, to be jealously guarded against all appropriations not sanctioned under the controls of the bourgeois knowledge factory. This is because within the context of the university the professor belongs to a definite class. The social position of the professor within the University is analogous to the petit-bourgeoisie within capitalist society - 'stuck between a rock and a hard place' unable to fight the management and bureaucracy of the university or to join with the students. The professor can do neither, because neither will benefit them.

VIII

'All social life is essentially practical'. Learning should (and can only really be) a practical activity. Students will learn more from getting together and becoming genuinely political (i.e. in critical practice) than from any book or lecture. The advantage of the university is that its schizophrenic self-image produces a space within society, a break from the rhythm of "work-life". This space can be used to write collectively, organise meetings in forgotten rooms, steal resources and exploit funding opportunities.

IX

The highest achievement of the university is the apparent freedom to criticise anything and everything. Until now this freedom has only been abstract, and has been ideologically compromised. Now is the time to take this critical freedom and make it happen.

X

The standpoint of the old university is the technocratic production of bourgeois subjectivity and the ideological construct of liberal democracy, a systematic fiction which we know attempts to hide a disgusting division of wealth and the daily exploitation of the many by the few.

The standpoint of the new university is a non-hierarchical, self-organised and directly political society for the production of revolutionary subjectivity. We can't know what this new society will look like, but we can only hope it will be nothing like the current one. Our strategy must be optimistic or it will be nothing.

X (and a half).

Universities and their academic acolytes have previously only talked about the world from a safe distance, basking in the glory of capitalist plaudits or else shrinking back embittered by their own inability to change material conditions.

The point is to live life, learn through it and change it, and in doing so change the world. To seize the production of knowledge from its specialised and moderated existence within various cycles of abstraction. The other point is that we might never have come to these conclusions without the existing university, this is what is wrong with the current situation and this is what has to be changed and overcome. We must destroy the old university and build a new one beyond its ruins.

Postscript.

Who are we? Students, we guess. At least, partly. Multiple voices, opinions and desires printed cheaply and stapled together at the spine. On second thoughts, who the fuck are you? Students we guess...? As an antidote to the institutional amnesia of the university - large numbers of brain cells flushed out to the job market and the job centre each year, as the new wave gurgles in - find here some profanities scratched onto cubicle walls. A partially drawn and badly conceived map of something we do not understand all the contours of, never could quite work out how all the partial views fitted together. The problems we face, the things that fuck us and fuck us off, things we wish we'd thought of earlier. If we have prevented just one child accepting lollipops from Michael Gove it will have all been worth it. Failing that, a door wedge is still a use value. Besides, we worked on it together and the work of engendering a collectivity is what is needed if we are to become the type of force capable of changing this entirely fucked and inherently unjust situation. Through a stroke of luck, it is also that collectivity which supplies the sustenance we need for this task. We have every faith that you are the person for the (hand)job.

www.studenthandjob.wordpress.com

Minor Compositions

Other titles in the series:
Precarious Rhapsody – Franco "Bifo" Berardi
Imaginal Machines – Stevphen Shukaitis
New Lines of Alliance, New Spaces of Liberty – Felix Guattari and Antonio Negri
The Occupation Cookbook
User's Guide to ~~Demanding~~ the Impossible – Laboratory of Insurrectionary Imagination
Spectacular Capitalism – Richard Gilman-Opalsky
Markets Not Capitalism – Ed. Gary Chartier & Charles W. Johnson
Revolutions in Reverse – David Graeber

Forthcoming:

Communization & its Discontents – Ed. Benjamin Noys
19 & 20 – Colectivo Situaciones
A Very Careful Strike – Precarias a la Deriva
Punkademics – Ed. Zack Furness
Art, Production and Social Movement – Ed. Gavin Grindon
The Soy Children – Eduardo Molinari
The [Open] Utopia – Thomas Moore & Stephen Duncombe

As well as a multitude to come…